pioneers of modern art

1 pablo picasso 1946

w. sandberg and h.l.c. jaffé

pioneers of modern art

in the museum of the city of amsterdam

translated by ian f.finlay

mcgraw-hill book company, inc., new york, toronto, london

this book was designed by w. sandberg
and printed in the netherlands by nv g. j. thieme, nijmegen
it was bound by proost & brandt nv amsterdam
the pictures have been made by the photo-staff of the
municipal museums of amsterdam; anefo (421); maria
austria (416); eva besnyö (438); louis van beurden (401);
jaap d'oliveira (5, 409, 410, 415, 426, 427); cas oorthuys (323, 324);
jan versnel (14, 15, 16, 134)
the plates were made by nv union amsterdam
the dustcover is a reproduction of a van gogh painting
and was printed by nv kunstdrukkerij vh j.a. luii & co
amsterdam

contents

une œuvre géniale,
qui commence par déconcerter
pourra créer peu à peu
par sa seule présence
une conception de l'art
et une atmosphère artistique
qui permettront de la comprendre

bergson, les deux sources 1932

it is not easy
to introduce this book
which looks so momentous

there is so much to say
so much has slipped my memory
during the long years
that I have concerned myself with
the relations between art and society

a museum is a place
where the community and art meet
and a museum of contemporary art
is a place where the community meets an art
with which it is not yet too familiar

what is the task of the artist:
to embellish life and render it more pleasant?
to help us towards beautiful thoughts?
to direct us away from the turmoil of the ordinary towards the sublime

or

to stand on the lookout with outstretched feelers
to taste what is coming
– long before we ordinary mortals are aware of it –

to go where life is most intense
where forces gather around a new birth
where new human relationships are ready to emerge
and to give them form, a face

for there are two kinds of artists
the first faithfully follows tradition
inspired by the work of great predecessors
they are many and form a school
they want to make "art" and manufacture paintings, sculptures
the second group may study the techniques of its predecessors but renews it
attempts to shape, to project what is growing
they do not talk about art
their works carry a message
they open our eyes

the first group of artists soothes, elevates, ennobles
we immediately call their work beautiful
and hang it up in the salon
the public is grateful and forgets them
the others shock us
we are struck, gripped, stimulated
or merely disconcerted
future generations, whose eyes have been opened
speak about their work in such terms as "beautiful" and "magnificent"
the history of art knows only this group
after their death, of course
they are then called "great artists"

great art is always an experiment

great artists are living now
they introduce us to the present
they prepare us for what is coming
their work is always topical
that is to say, they are continually growing

look at our own time:
wars are rapids in history

economic relations change faster
barriers between groups fade
prejudices disappear
far away peoples gain freedom

but these basic changes
have their repercussions on social institutions
as yet unfound
new life, often wild, is seen of course in youth
and in art

rock 'n roll, blue jeans,
blousons noirs, halbstarken
nozems

action painting, l'art informel
un art autre, experimental art
abstract expressionism
have put a stop to the legend of the "fine arts"
the artist plunges with abandon into the unknown
in order to render visible, palpable, audible, perceptible
the new, the life which is approaching

true art is, at its birth, exacting and ill-bred
does not speak, but shouts

our museum has seen it as its duty
to confront the public with it again and again

holland, at the intersection of north and south, east and west
has its own task
young artists understood it
* copenhagen, brussels, amsterdam   the "cobra" group
in 1949 brings together artists
from america, the netherlands, germany, hungary
denmark, belgium, france
works by karel appel, constant, corneille
asger jorn, tajiri, césar, alechinsky, lucebert
shock the visitor

one speaks of scandal

our museum continues without looking back
along that path
it tries to show everything
which can offer a contribution
towards the shaping of this age

what is now coming into existence
but also the recent past
the whole renaissance of the twentieth century:
the bauhaus
futurism, constructivism, the stijl
cubism, fauvism, expressionism
and of course the fathers of that renaissance:
cézanne, monet, gauguin, vincent van gogh -

vincent, the lowliest, most human
of these four, realizes
the new relation between man and man
which is busy growing
liberté, égalité, fraternité   he depicts the equality and fraternity
which are the roots of freedom

sandberg

'60-'45

a after the war

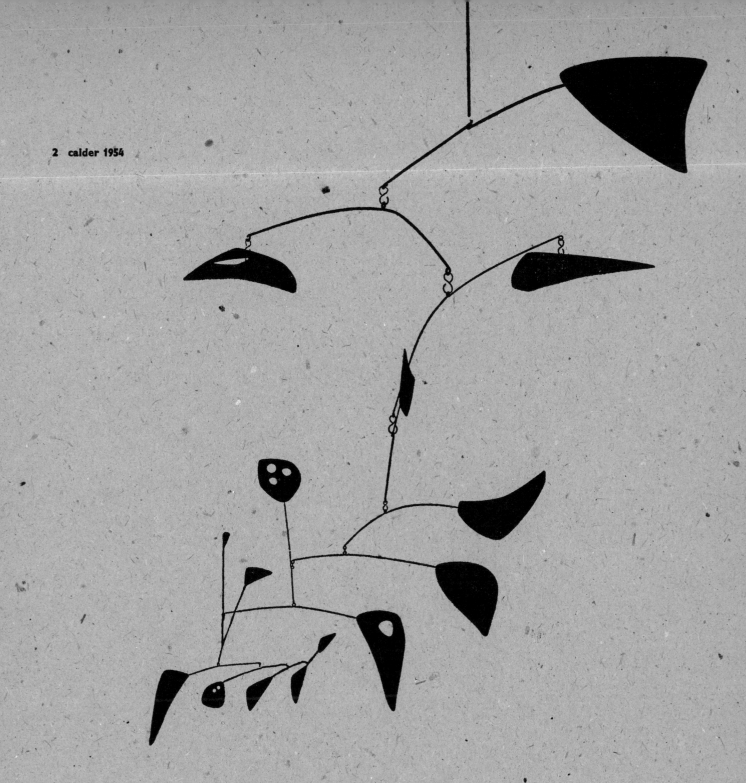

photography, chair, tapestry and film

3 photo f. l. lemaire 1957

4 photo ed van der elsken 1950

5   gerrit + wim rietveld 1957

6   1957   7   1943

12   13

14   15

16   friso kramer 1958

gerrit rietveld

8 **1936**   9 **1935**   10 **1923**   11 **1920**

van sliedregt

17 gerrit rietveld 1918

18

19

20

21

18   victor devasarely 1950
19   ria van oerle 1951
20   ida kerkovius 1954
21   roger bissière 1945

22

26

27

23

28

31

24

29

32

30

25

33

contemporary art in the collection

*S'il est vrai que toute histoire
est l'interprétation actuelle du
passé, la conscience de l'art actuel
est la base de toute histoire de
l'art du passé*

L. Venturi

"The museum for contemporary art has its origin in the present and then proceeds step by step back into the past." The catalogue which surveys the acquisitions and activities of the Municipal Museum of Amsterdam (the Stedelijk Museum) during the nine years after the war begins with the above words, which are in the nature of a program. These same words may, with even more justification, be placed at the beginning of a publication which—seven years later—reviews the sixty-five-year history of the Museum. We may view the works of art which give this Museum its importance from the same point from which we also look back on the history of these sixty-five years, namely from the present.

The aim of a museum of contemporary art is, after all, to help in making us aware of our own epoch. It is the desire of the contemporary museum to hold a mirror in front of people living today, in which they can see and recognize themselves—and it is not surprising that this recognition should sometimes be accompanied by feelings of alarm and resentment. A museum for modern art must however always proceed from our own reality; the partner in the imaginary conversation which takes place in the rooms of the museum is our contemporary, the person living today.

For this reason, the history of art in a museum for modern art will also begin in the present. We cannot represent contemporary art deterministically as the result of generations of artists; on the contrary, we will, starting from the present, have to attempt to sketch the pedigree of this art. And such a pedigree is, for living art, by no means merely an enumeration of facts gleaned from artistic vital statistics; more significant than the actual family relationships are often the "Wahlverwandschaften" (or elective affinities), and a generation of artists often feels itself more closely related to its artistic grandfathers than to the masters from whose school they came. There will, in every family, be a living descendant who suddenly discovers a resemblance connecting him with a great-uncle or a great-grandfather—and then only will he wish to know

more about that ancestor, more also about his other great-uncles or great-grandparents. These are the foundations on which we attempt to sketch the pedigree of contemporary art. We must not, however, lose sight of artistic vital statistics; but we must also not forget that we are dealing with living art and living artists. The pedigree of every living person is not merely an objective fact, but above all the source of a subjective choice. Here he can choose his ideals, his examples, here he can enrich or consolidate his personality. He will, however, do that through his own choice and through the choice which his own epoch imposes upon him.

This is true particularly of the artist, who does perhaps inherit his language from an earlier generation, but who always draws his inspiration from the life around him, from the society of which he forms part. He will form his own tradition from the facts of his pedigree—for a tradition becomes significant only when it is verified again by natural choice.

Contemporary art appears in this way as a collection of works, each of which rests on its own pedigree, its own tradition. The highest common factor in this multiplicity of individual works would then be the phenomenon we are going to call the style of a period. It is difficult to define this style, but as the observer compares a series of works from one period with the products of another, the unity of each period will be apparent almost immediately. In every historically defined period—and the natural boundaries are in our century unfortunately the wars—artists are faced collectively with the same problems. These problems concern not merely painting as such—they affect not only the painter, the sculptor and their subject, but the human being, the artist. They have therefore—particularly in this century—the same validity independently of the place where they arise. This survey of the collection of the Municipal Museum of Amsterdam may therefore also be divided into chapters which correspond to the periods of our most recent history.

The image which this division presents to the observer's eye is nevertheless more complicated than would appear at first sight. The problems of art are, of course, set by a historical situation, by the specific character of a period, but the language in which artists will answer this question will vary enormously. This is not only as a result of the nature of the country, or of the individual character of the various artists, but the main reason for the differences will be found to depend on their dates of birth. Although the problem in the visual arts is a matter of general human validity, the language of artists has an autonomous development contained in the subject. This development takes place—as does any evolution—in succeeding generations. Whereas the stating of the problem in art may therefore change abruptly, in a revolutionary manner through sudden shocks in human society, the development of imaginative language will always change gradually from generation to generation, from master to pupil.

In this way there arises in the picture of the development of the visual arts a polyphony, which we also know from a pedigree. Generations telescope into one another, a young descendant from one generation resembles his grandfather more than he does his father, and is quite unlike his brothers, the pupils of one and the same artist . . . Various generations are at work at the same time—just as members of various generations work together in one attorney's office—and are confronted with the same problems dictated by time. Their approach to these problems will nevertheless differ—must in fact differ—because of the differences in their dates of birth. What for the young artist is an initial triumph over his difficulties, is for the older one sometimes a swan song.

Modern art is consequently a richly variegated score, with many parts, and not a simple monophonic melody. And each part—which has its point of entry and exit—contributes to the richness of the whole, each part carries with it something from the past, as a result of which it can enrich the present.

A contemporary museum confronts those living today with the facts of today and with their pedigree, seen with the eyes of the contemporary. It can thus contribute to an awareness of our own time, and to the realization that contemporary art is calling to us: tua res agitur.

34 theo wolvecamp 1956

painting

35   karel appel 1953

36   karel appel 1957

37 **1949**

karel appel

38 **1948**

39 **1953**

40   karel appel 1953

43

41

44

42

41 lucebert 1959
42 constant 1951
43 constant 1951
44 jaap nanninga 1957
45 corneille 1959

45

46

ger lataster 1959

47

48   ger lataster 1957

49

gerrit benner 1954

50

a the art of today: the period after the war

The art of today is faced with a completely novel situation: all the certainties which had formed a firm foundation for earlier generations have turned out to be illusions or apparent certainties. The bearers of this art—the artists—are also members of a society which is likewise seeking its way by groping in the midst of certainties which have grown moldy or have been overthrown. These artists have lived through one or two world wars, they have seen how the values which were dearest to them have been trampled underfoot, and yet continued to retain their value; they have seen how, under Nazi dictatorship, art, which had still remained true amidst all that deception, was put under a ban, while shoddy work had to take its place . . . And nevertheless, precisely because of this, they continued to express the life of their epoch, to render this invisible life visible. In common with every art, they want to communicate, i.e., they want the observer to share in the artist's experience.

As a result of the position of visual art in our age, however, that communication has had to assume a new form. The message of modern art, its language and its public, have all become fraught with problems. There is no longer any item—such as the words of the Holy Scriptures in the Middle Ages—which brings both the artist and the spectator together. There is no longer any language which—like that of reality in the nineteenth century—is spoken by the artist and understood by his public; and finally, there is no longer even a well-defined public to which the artist today knows he is connected, such as was still the case with the 19th-century portrait painter, who knew he was attached to the middle classes who commissioned him. And yet present-day artists turn in some cases to an imaginary public: they speak a language which is comprehended by some and which is experienced by many and understood as music (which does say "something" to us too), and they attempt to convince those who are willing to look at their work of the truth of the message they propagate.

They are, however, again and again reproached with being unintelligible—the fact that their work is a seeking, an experiment, is used as an argument against contemporary art. But it cannot be otherwise. Living artists realize only too well that it is impossible to perpetuate an old tradition in the midst of a new situation, in the midst of so many certainties which have since passed away. It would be wrong to transfer the apparent certainties of the 19th century to our own and to construct an art upon them expressing contemporary life—a life which no longer knows those

certainties and which has, by its own experience, not yet found new, future certainties.

The main certainty on which all art and the whole of tradition up to the beginning of this century and a long way into it was built was the acceptance of external, visible reality. Every painting was, up to the end of the 19th century also partly a document, an announcement concerning the facts of this reality. The decay of this foundation of the visual arts resulted from the invention and perfection of photography and the film. Man now had for the first time another possibility for capturing reality and immortalizing it. Those who wished to possess a portrait, a memory of a person, a landscape, a house, or an animal, no longer had to consult the painter, but could do as well at the photographer's. Thus there occurred, precisely in visual art, a shifting of the accent, a new orientation. No longer the perpetuation of the visible natural form, but the capturing of even the most transient visions of reality is now the aim of artists—they try to render visible precisely the invisible element in reality, to give expression to the forces and laws which, veiled or hidden, live in and beyond the phenomena of nature. As a result of the rise of the technical image of reality, painting is experiencing its industrial revolution. Reality has, however, also changed for the artist in another respect; as a result of scientific discoveries, the idea of reality has also been modified. Space and time are no longer firm and immutable unities; reality itself, as perceived by our senses, has become problematic. Artists try to render visible the forces which are at work behind perceptible reality. Painting here shares in the general revolution which has been brought about by science in our view of nature. For this reason, too, its works have become experiments.

Liberated in this way from an old and beloved task, the depiction of reality, and confronted by a new situation—without a generally valid message, without a generally accepted language, and without any closely defined public—contemporary art nevertheless attempts to express the atmosphere of the life of our time. The feelings and thoughts on which contemporary artists confer form will therefore lie principally on the level of general values, being the highest common factor of the diverging ideologies which surround the artist in our age. Since no general form has been found for these—invisible—subjects, their various expressions will again and again bear the character of an experiment, of a searching for a compelling and convincing form. Bearing in mind the rich variety of origin, type of country and temperament of contemporary artists, the results of these experiments will differ greatly; nevertheless, they all share an experimental quality.

In the case of these living artists, inspiration for a work comes from very varied aspects of life; sometimes it is the structure of the simplest living organisms which captivates the artist, then again the strictly conceived mechanical components of a technical age, or possibly the decay and decomposition which artists—and all of us—perceive in our contemporary society and its products. They are, however, always expressions of an age "in which our views concerning reality are changing, in which the inexpressible acquires form, and in which what takes place in the human brain and heart suddenly appears more important than what can be perceived by the senses." (Fierens).

This change therefore occurs in all countries, and especially in those which have experienced the shock of the war. Everywhere there is a revival of violence, borne by a young generation which puts its faith in the spontaneity, the violence, of its immediate feelings. Bodily movement, the vividness of the gesture, interpret the inner turbulence of the artist; the occasionally aggressive force of the gesture becomes clear in large-scale works. This trend has appeared in America as action painting, but a similar fierceness can also be discerned in other countries as well. The young generation here invokes Kandinsky, Klee, Miró and Max Ernst as its predecessors, because it was precisely these artists who brought spontaneous writing into effect. This new, postwar art also took root in the Netherlands, and certain Dutch artists are among the leaders of this— essentially romantic—movement. Many too are the expressions of contemporary art which are grouped together in the museum's collection to form a whole. In the case of the Dutch artists, there is a common tendency towards the expressive, which is also evident here and there

36-40 in the work of foreign artists. *Appel*'s large colored compositions are a testimony to the vitality with which the artist approaches and interprets reality; the force and turbulence of his forms and colors are an expression of man's need at the present time to communicate his own

49 dynamic feelings to his surroundings. *Benner*'s work forms a contrast by the joyful tranquillity with which the painter looks at and listens to the world, the childlike happiness with which a simple person views what he calls the mysterious

45 world. The canvases of *Corneille* originate from a different attitude towards the world. The painter wishes to arrange his mature impressions and memories, after intensive

penetration, in a significant and captivating pattern. These canvases express a poetic feeling. Finally, in *Ouborg*'s work, **65** we find great spontaneity, combined with a thoroughly introspective contemplation. His canvases show quite distinctly that visionary, dreamlike element which finds its material in the interplay of colors and lines, as they loom up before our closed eyes. The contribution of Dutch painters to this new trend nevertheless forms only a part of the wider aspect of postwar painting. The Dutch are full representatives of this art, but there are also related artists in other countries.

The works of foreign artists provide a similar picture, although the expressive element is not always so pronounced in their case. *Pollock*'s *Water Bull* and *Jorn*'s paintings are **56-60** related to Ouborg's spontaneous writing and Appel's vital means of expression. The composition by *Bissière*—the **71** teacher of a whole generation of young French painters— shows the same introspective, poetic view as the work of many Dutch artists. Indeed, a new feeling of life began to inspire people all over the world after the war—a feeling which has found arresting expression in works of music and poetry as well as of visual art. It is an attitude of violent, rebellious revolt, which rejects and reviles not only every discipline, but also the very thought of harmony and conventional beauty. For the world of today, with its fears, its oppressions, and also its clumsy attempts to create order, does not seem to give any cause for seeking harmony, but rather for a violent protest, a tormented cry which will care little about what key the cry begins in.

Such a cry is spontaneous and aggressive, and these attitudes are also characteristic of contemporary art. Colors and forms encounter one another stridently and piercingly, the brushstroke is hurried and feverish—everything contributes to conferring upon the work a construction, tense vividness, the character of a revolt which abominates every semblance of classical tranquillity, of contemplative reflection. The vivid, challenging gesture replaces the controlled stroke; the piercing dissonance is more suited to interpreting revolt than is an elaborate harmony. Freedom of expression, and also of movement and construction, appear as the first characteristic of all these works. This craving for freedom —a clearly romantic trait—reveals a new feeling towards life, which contrasts violently with the classical search for objective standards. The subjectivity which stamps each

Note: Marginal numbers accompanying this text refer to works of art reproduced in this book and numbered in sequence from 1 through 444. Full information on each work may be found at the end of the book.

51   bram van velde 1959

↑ 52 gea panter 1960   53 josef zaritsky 1946 →

← 55   roger hilton 1953   54   alan davie 1956 ↑

56　jackson pollock 1945　　57　kimber smith 1958

58   pablo picasso 1946

59   marc chagall 1947

work of art as a personal expression, as an explosive testimony, stresses the individual character of every work; but this subjectivism is at the same time also the highest common factor in contemporary art, and therefore causes contemporary works to resemble one another closely, in spite of their individual differences. This feature is evident not only in the works of the younger generation, but also just as much in the paintings by the older masters, some of whom are now over seventy.

46   Besides Appel in the Netherlands, *Lataster* is certainly one of the most convincing representatives of this movement, which has as its adherents in other countries, *inter alia*, the

60-57   Dane *Asger Jorn* and *Kimber Smith,* who lives in Paris and has succeeded in adding the large-scale American dimension to this trend in painting. Likewise the recent large gouaches

58   by *Bram van Velde*—a Dutchman living in Paris—show the characteristic of spontaneous subjectivity, of freedom of expression and treatment of paint. And alongside these blazing, vivid canvases, the protest and revolt are also revealed in another type of work, as in the mocking,

61   satirical canvases of *Dubuffet* and—in the Netherlands—the

67   works of *Wagemaker* which, although refined, are sometimes rendered oppressive by their material. The difference between a previous period—and a preceding generation—

75   becomes particularly clear also in *Poliakoff*'s abstract compositions, in which free forms that have evolved from the feeling of the maker have replaced the regularity of the geometrical limitations of former days. Whereas before the war expression was given to the harmony of mathematics and lawfulness, this has now been replaced by the demonic nature of a new—romantic—attitude to life. This change in human demeanor is perhaps most clearly seen in the work of the masters of an older generation—the masters who formulated their language at the beginning of this century, but who now interpret in that language their answer to the

190   problems of today. *Picasso's Woman in a Fish Hat,* painted in 1942 during the Second World War, is perhaps the most striking example of this change. The tragedy and demonic element of the present-day world are expressed here by means that date from a former epoch, but are handled with a greater freedom, with the force of a subjective testimony. The same shift towards a more expressive vision also

59-74   characterizes the post war works of *Chagall, Baumeister,* and *Léger;* even in countries such as Israel, where a national art has been emerging only since the founding of this young

76   state, we find this phenomenon, as may be seen in *Ardon's* recent works.

Besides painting, we must also mention other forms of

expression which are typical of our age. The painting, the small mobile canvas or panel in a frame, has in the present crisis of art and society itself become a problem. Painting nevertheless continues. It has, however, in recent years turned more and more to other forms, which do not have to such an extent the all too individual or experimental character of a painting and which play a greater social role. In the Netherlands the predominating form for this new trend in painting is graphic art, which has recently under-

97-105   gone a revival in our country. Prints by *Heyboer, Lucebert,*

101   and *Ten Holt* are examples of the riches collected in our section devoted to the graphic arts. Apart from the work of these Dutch artists, that of several other European countries is also represented in this part of the collection. Work dating from the postwar years is, however, always characterized by the same attitude of mind; the stroke, the hand, has acquired more freedom, and a print or drawing dating from this period differs from one from the prewar years by its greater sense of movement and vividness. The

118-114   work of *Hartung* and of *Soulages* typifies this trend, of which

125   *Miró* is often regarded as the forerunner. The magnificent

122   expressionistic woodcuts by *Grieshaber* differ from the work of his predecessors precisely in this freedom, and the late work of Chagall—compared with his earlier prints—shows these same characteristics.

In the Netherlands and elsewhere this new striving in painting is directed less to the individual and his home —where the new Dutch examples of graphic art find their main outlet—but rather to a community. Mural paintings and woven carpets are intended to attract the attention of people assembled in public buildings. The woven wall

21-20   covers of Le Corbusier, *Bissière* and *Ida Kerkovius* show clearly a strong link with architecture; through their effect they strengthen the character of the wall as a plane and also add to it the harmony of their color. Le Corbusier's graphically touching work breathes a lofty tranquillity, while the carpets of Bissière and Ida Kerkovius attain, through the effect of their material, a scintillating play-fulness which enlivens the plane.

Finally, a word about present-day sculpture. It shows the same varied nature as the other branches of living art.

97   Tajiri's small *Sculpture* suggests, through the playfulness of its plastic, interweaving lines, an example of graphic art in

77   space. Germaine Richier has been inspired in her *Storm* by the gruesome decay, the dissolution of many features, of our society, and has given them a suggestive form using a

78   suitable technique. The figures of the Dutchman *Couzijn*

60   asger jorn ±1954

61   jean dubuffet 1957

62 jean dubuffet 1957

63

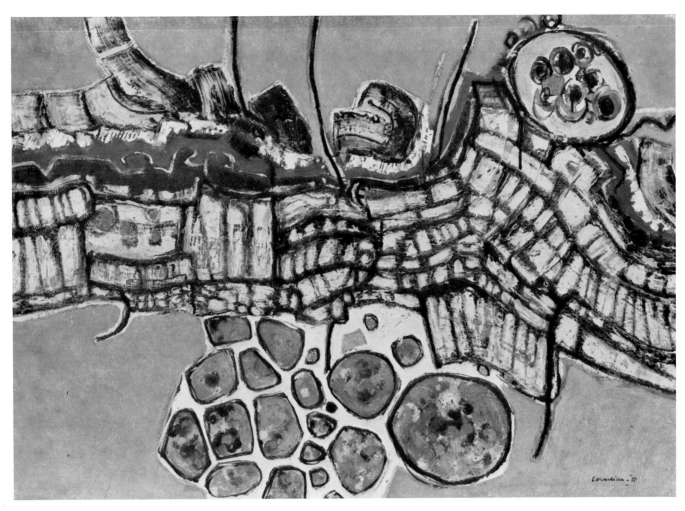

64

65

66

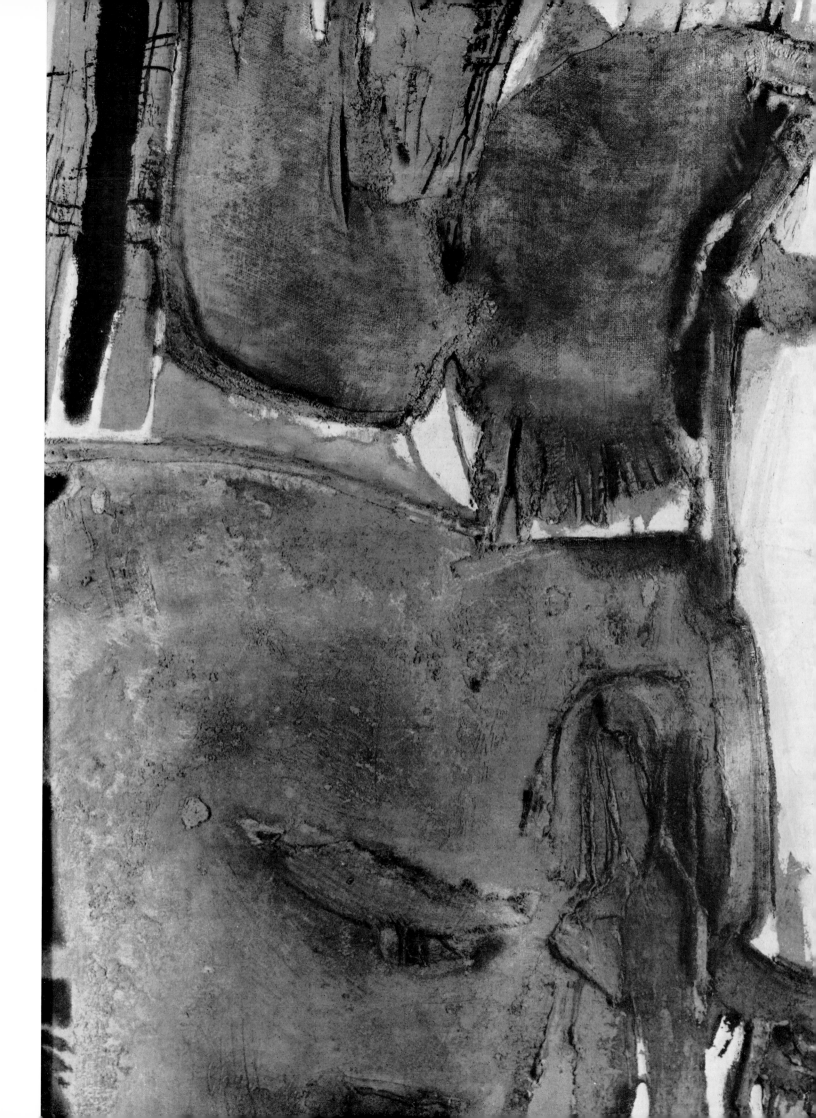

69 gerrit benner 1958
70 theo wolvecamp 1959
71 roger bissière 1952
72 roger bissière 1951

69

70

71

72

73   vieira da silva 1954

74   willi baumeister 1942

75   serge poliakoff ±1952   76 mordecaï ardon 1956

show a dramatic sense of feeling which the visitor to the
museum will know from contemporary painting, but which
he also finds in the figures of *Marino Marini* and *Henry Moore*.   92-93
The capricious feeling of contemporary sculpture is clearly
based on a baroque origin in *Étienne-Martin's Homage to*   82
Bernini—the exuberant movement of the work has its
origin in a violently gesticulating tree stump. The difference
between this and work of an earlier period is typical. If a
sculptor then began from a "found object", he chose for
it the sound forms of a stone polished by water, of a crystal
formed regularly by nature. The work of masters of the
prewar generation in our collection—*Gabo* and *Pevsner*—   87-86
shows the difference clearly. In the development of the
work of *Jacobsen*, this shift from regularity to turbulence is   91
evident in one man's output. Alexander Calder has also
created a completely new plastic form, a form which is
therefore so typical of our generation, because it inter-
weaves time and space. His *Mobile* is a plastic mass, which   2
moves, and is consequently no longer a stationary object,
but an everchanging form, an ensemble of plastic movement
and the dance, a development in space, and therefore such
a vivid interpretation of our present-day view of life, which
is characterized by the dynamic nature of forms, an
expression of a (romantic) revolt against the apparent
order of this age, an expression also of the will of this
generation to confer again a greater validity on subjective
values—just as with "personal politics".

sculpture

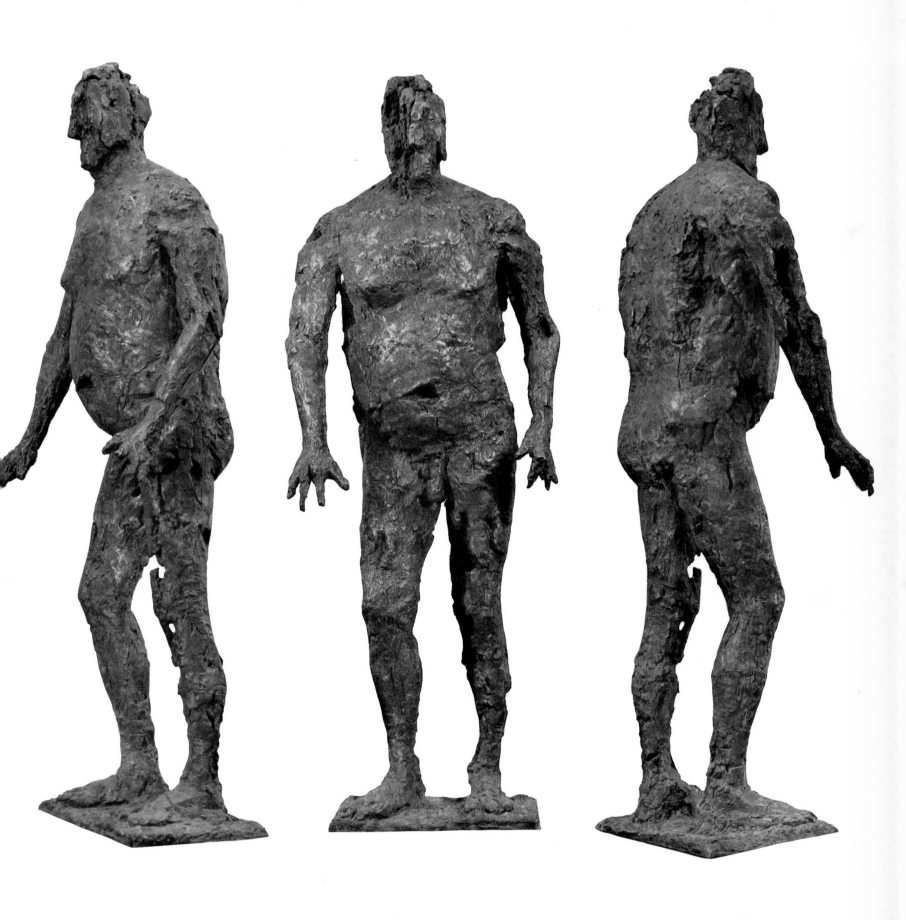

77   germaine richier ±1948

78 couzijn 1958

79

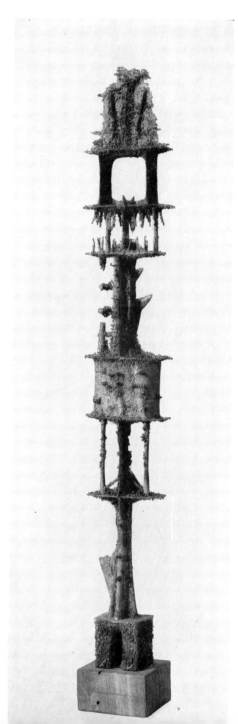

80

tajiri ±1952-57

81

82   henri etienne-martin 1957

carel visser 1954

83

84

85

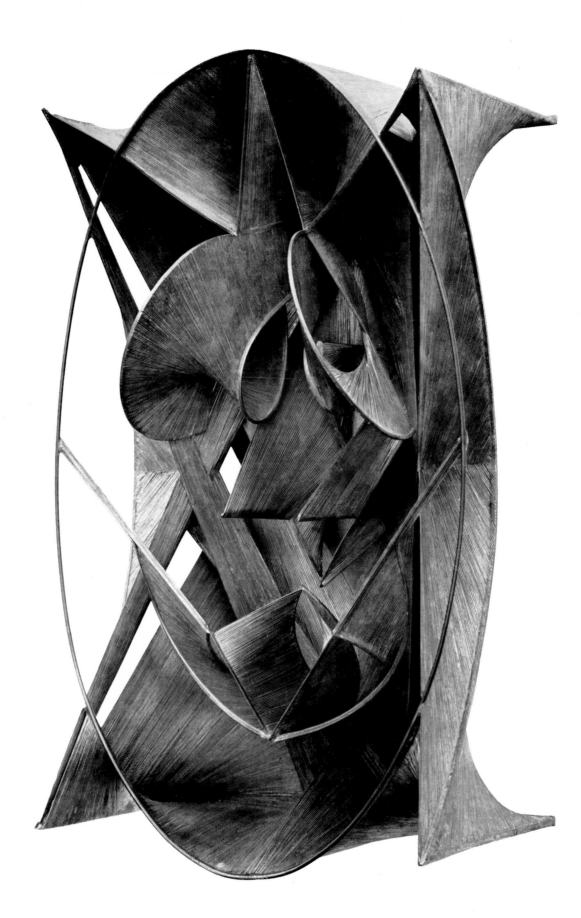

86   antoine pevsner 1945

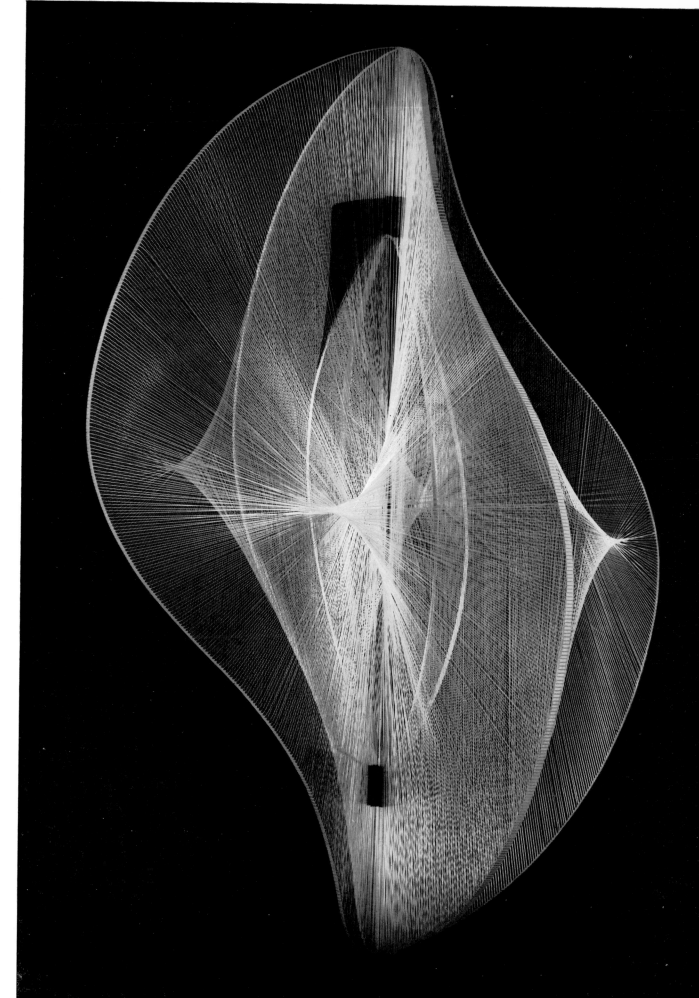

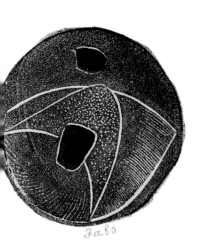

89

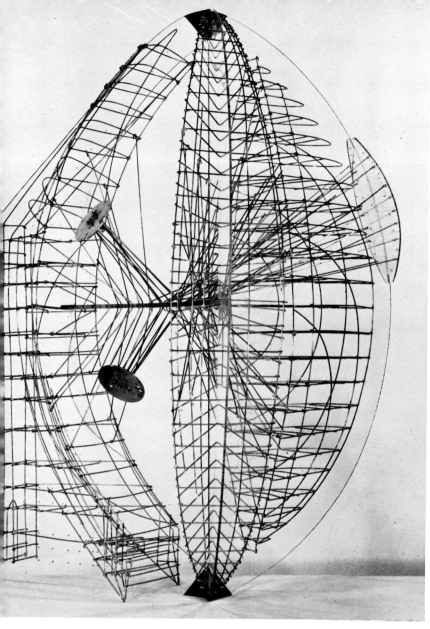

90

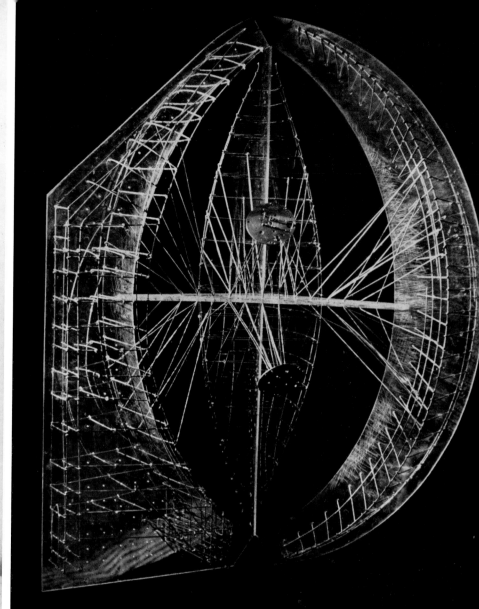

89 andré volten 1956
90 constant 1955
91 robert jacobsen 1952

91

92 marino marini 1947   93 henri moore 1957 ⬇

graphic arts

94 wagemaker 1956

95 fassbender ±1950

96 mucchi 1944

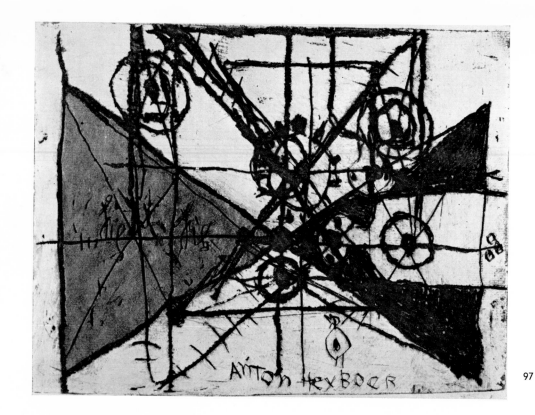

97

98

97 anton heyboer 1957
98 anton heyboer 1957
99 anton heyboer 1957
100 ger lataster 1954
101 friso ten holt 1953
102 asger jorn 1953
103 asger jorn 1953
104 asger jorn 1952

99

10

100

101

103

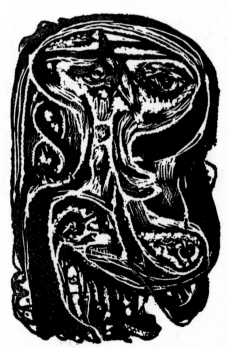

104

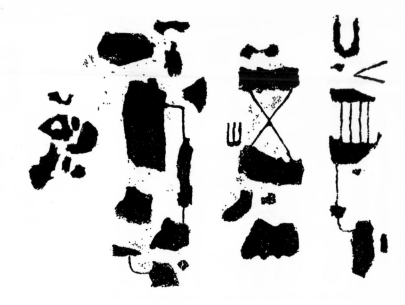

110

105

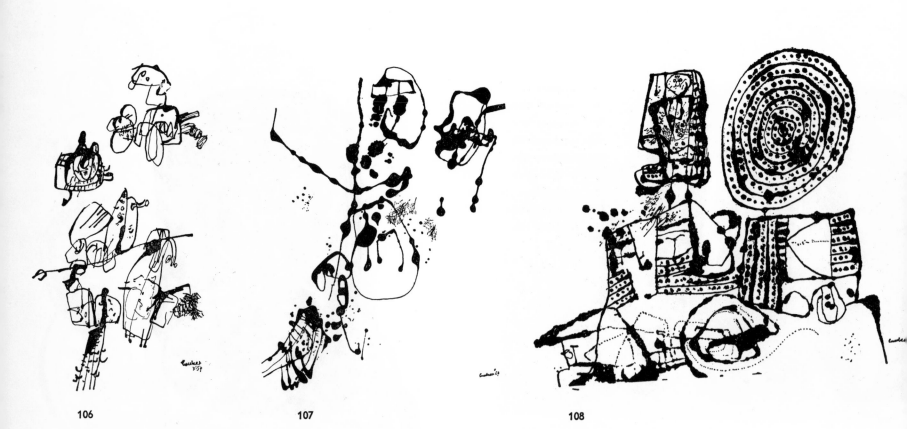

106

107

108

111

112

105   lucebert 1957
106   lucebert 1957
107   lucebert 1957
108   lucebert 1958
109   lucebert 1958
110   willi baumeister ± 1951
111   willi baumeister ± 1951
112   willi baumeister ± 1952
113   corneille 1954

109

113

114

114 ben nicholson 1948
115 pierre soulages 1957
116 h. g. adam 1952
117 carel visser 1955

115

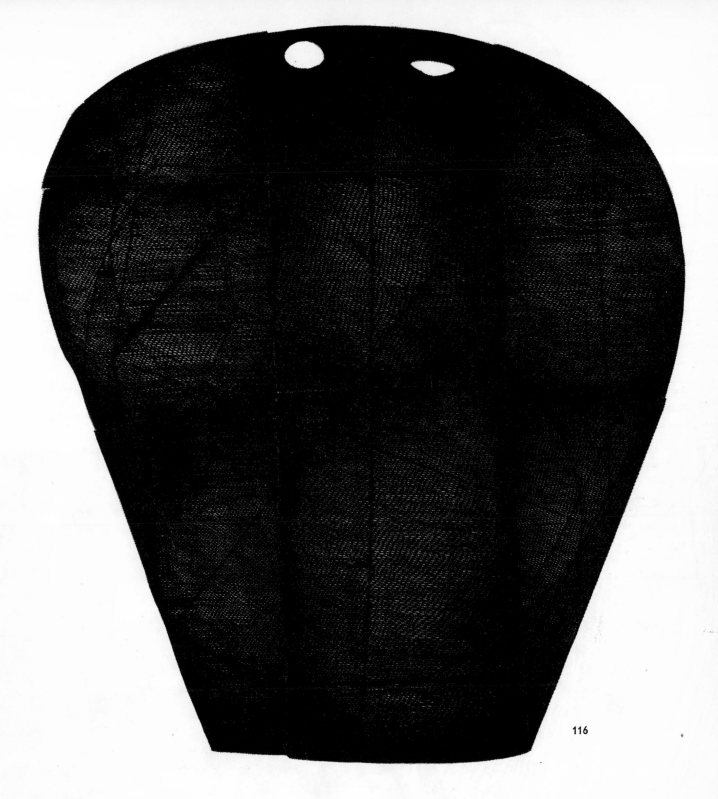

116

117

118

118   hans hartung ± 1953
119   ch. roelofsz
120   ch. roelofsz
121   ben shahn ± 1958

IF IT HAD NOT BEEN FOR THESE THING,
I MIGHT HAVE LIVE OUT MY LIFE TALK-
ING AT STREET CORNERS TO SCORN-
ING MEN. I MIGHT HAVE DIE, UN-
MARKED, UNKNOWN, A FAILURE. NOW
WE ARE NOT A FAILURE. THIS IS OUR
CAREER AND OUR TRIUMPH. NEVER IN
OUR FULL LIFE COULD WE HOPE TO
DO SUCH WORK FOR TOLERANCE, FOR
JOOSTICE, FOR MAN'S ONDERSTANDING
OF MAN AS NOW WE DO BY ACCIDENT.
OUR WORDS-OUR LIVES-OUR PAINS
NOTHING! THE TAKING OF OUR LIVES-
LIVES OF A GOOD SHOEMAKER AND A
POOR FISH PEDDLER-ALL! THAT LAST
MOMENT BELONGS TO US- THAT
AGONY IS OUR TRIUMPH.

121

119

120

122 grieshaber

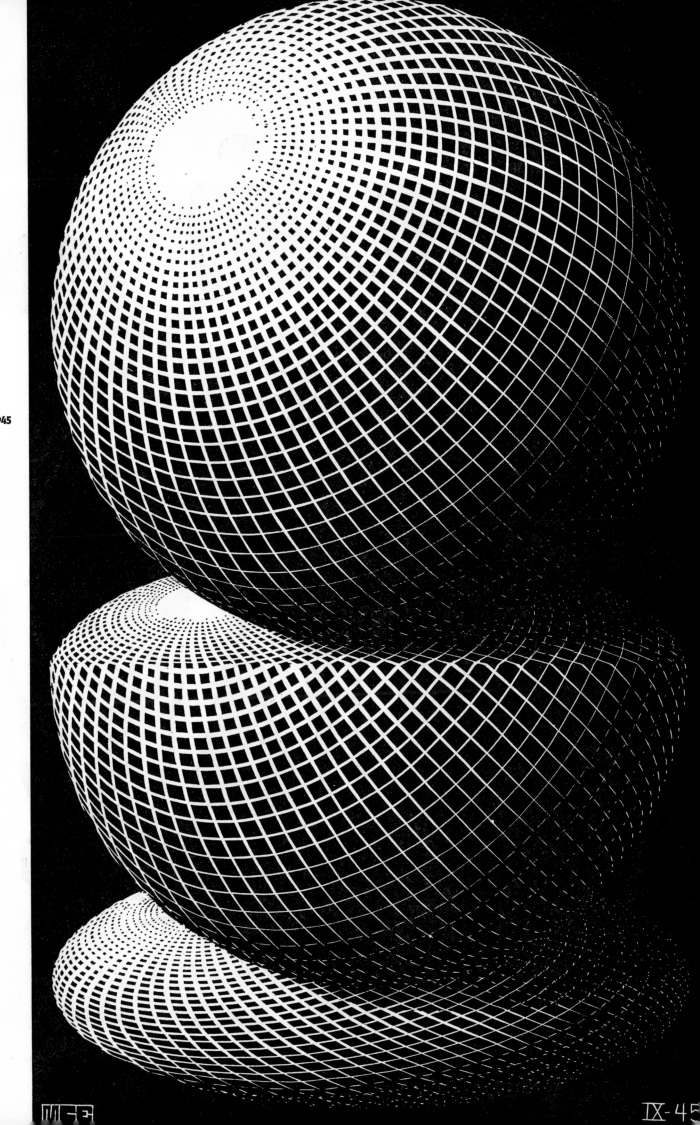

123 m. c. escher 1945

124 fernand léger 1950

Il faut voir de près

Les curieux

Quand on s'ennuie.

125   joan mirò 1958

126 matisse 1947

Wie biedt? Wat baat mij de stapelplaats
janmaats en machinegeweren? Wie biedt meer,
biedt mij een plaats zonder praatjes
van maan, mooie mogol of moloch of mammon,
een gewone plek zon, zonder gouden verleden?
Magnaat, magistraat, advocaat van de duivel,
wie biedt? En ik vraag geen afbraak.

Zij hebben octrooi op instortende huizen
en kleerscheuren, alleenvertoningsrecht
van mijn regen, op de rechte weg
de tol, om mijn geld te geven, te heffen,
het vruchtgebruik van gewassen:
koolzaad en graan en de zoete peen.

ne se touchant pas mais
à des distances en chaque

seconde différentes
De même

'40-'18

b between two wars

b between two wars

Looking back from the present to prewar art, we must be struck immediately by the great change in spiritual climate. The characteristic feature of visual art today is on all sides the experiment, the search for new forms, the groping for an expression of our attitude towards life, which can no longer find embodiment in traditional forms. Contemporary artists attempt to interpret the world outside and inside themselves, such as they, children of our time, see it. They often avoid perceptible reality; in most cases, however, they seek a general rhythm behind its phenomena, a harmony connecting everything, or they shout out their protest against this reality with violent gestures.

In the Thirties, that is to say before the war, it was not the search for new solutions that was characteristic of the art of the period—oppression left its mark on all artists and their works. That is why the reality expressed in their canvases has such a completely different character from that which had ever existed before. The painters of the Thirties, particularly in the Netherlands, see reality not, as did 19th-century painters, as a piece of living nature which they perceive and record. They see that reality as a frightening, often alarming, and sometimes softening combination of strange, hostile elements. Their efforts are directed towards characterizing these elements in all their strangeness and in holding the oppression which they radiate. The things which constitute (or appear to constitute) the subject matter of these works are nothing but the writing on the wall.

In all parts of the world visual art in the Thirties expressed the oppression, the fear, of this age in a similar way. The German *neue Sachlichkeit* with *Otto Dix* and *George Grosz* is just as much a reflection of it as surrealism, which portrayed the absurdity of a hostile world. The development in the Netherlands presents a different picture compared with these international movements. Our country was not involved in the First World War, and had been spared the main shock that occurred in the first decades of this century. The oppression of the Thirties had therefore to be expressed here in a different way. It was not so much the absurd, the fantastic, which shocked people's minds in the Netherlands—it was things themselves, in their hard, pitiless hostility, which interpreted the evil message.

The direction in Dutch painting represented by *Willink*, *Hynckes* and others has often been called "magic realism." The remarkable thing about these works, which are built up from observations of existing reality, is precisely their

unreal atmosphere, their oppressive stillness, the calm before the storm. A series of *self-portraits* by these artists shows this oppressive view of the world, even on their own faces. In prewar years things did in fact speak to most artists in a language of fear and chilliness, and objectivity consequently meant to the artist the feeling and experiencing of the gulf between himself and every thing, person, and object outside himself—being at the same time a realization of the hostility and stillness of every thing, every "affair", which he saw and felt. This objective, but principally oppressive and chilling, manner of looking at the external world is found not only in the Netherlands, since Stanley Spencer's *self-portrait* also reflects it particularly well. There is, however, also another type of objectivity, namely that with which *Dick Ket* approaches things. His technique is just as careful and precise, his coloring just as sober, as that of the magic realists. His attitude to things is, however, quite different. He follows every detail of the thing, the "affair", which confronts him with an almost devout attention. The simplest objects, which he prefers to paint, such as a flower pot, a tea towel, a jug, fill his whole painting, and they also fill his world. He surrenders with a *devotio moderna* to these simple objects, and his objectivity thus becomes an expression of his alliance to these humble things which alone have preserved their completeness in the midst of a threatening world. He has also drawn his *self-portrait* with that same objective surrender, without pathos and finery.

In his surrender to things, in his modest auscultation of their nature, and in his constantly new admiration of their richness of form, Ket is related to the "Sunday Painters". Their work also proceeds from a modest surrender to nature and that is why it differs so much from 19th-century naturalism, which thought it could compete with nature. The Sunday Painters, or present-day primitives, practice their art in their spare time and find relaxation in the sometimes clumsy, but precise and candid, reproducing of what they see before their eyes.

The art of Charley Toorop is, in essence, related to this attitude, which we call primitive, because we ourselves can no longer combine an objective view with living with things themselves. It is, however, principally the monumentality which she succeeds in achieving that causes her work to rise above other similar expressions of prewar "objectivity" Her *Cheese Market at Alkmaar* is a masterpiece of Dutch art in the Thirties, precisely because she succeeds in

206-10

205

212

168

211
208

198

raising the objective material above its chance nature and in conferring upon it an impressive monumentality. The figures in this painting seem, with their healthy strength, to burst out of the frame; the large, round cheeses become through their volume and weight the center of the work, which seems to be constructed from heavy spheres—the cheeses and the bony bodies of the carriers.
Charley Toorop thus brings an order into her paintings—and into her world. In common with the Sunday Painters, her work has a directness of approach, a sympathy with which every object is observed; it is related to magic realism by the hard, unsentimental shaping which allows every object to be an object. The strength of portrayal, however, the monumentality, as a result of which each object seems larger, larger often than its form as perceived, but not too large in terms of its significance—that is the achievement of the painter. In the postwar years she has succeeded in raising this sober strength and monumentality to a higher degree of tension—a few still lifes of fruit and everyday objects being proof of this. The oppression expressed in the works of the magic realists occasionally looms up in these works, but then it is another sound we hear, namely the abhorrence of so much cruelty and destruction, the cry of revolt against the enfeebling and tarnishing of object and man—the object and man which Charley Toorop wishes to show precisely in their strength and dignity.

What does the art of "new objectivity"—preeminently the art of the Thirties—mean to us today in the 1960's?
Much of its importance lies in the fact that artists in those years predicted the coming war and approaching inhumanity. The oppression expressed by their works was, a few years later, to become reality, in fact, a much worse reality; but the mood, the fear, the desperation, had already been portrayed in the works of that period. The view of life in the Thirties, which was under the spell of a continual threat, has through these artists become a visible sign. The oppressive feeling which proceeds from their works has its origin principally in the things depicted, which stand there side by side—hard, lonely and dehumanized. The events of the approaching war showed that the artists had, for the most part, been correct. The horror of the war years was often one of the things which came to confront us hostilely and ferociously.
After the war, when fear and oppression could recede, this form of painting lost much of its significance. Yet many of its technical advances passed over into postwar art, notably an unsentimental, cogent manner of seeing things. A few

artists—principally Charley Toorop in the Netherlands—have directed the technical and visual acquisitions of the prewar years to a new domain. Our view of reality, at the present time is liberated from the pressure which weighed upon it in the Thirties. The paintings of those years have nevertheless helped us to see the things in the world around us more cogently, objectively, and clearly. Any form of realism which desires in our time to present a picture of the world and its mood links up with much of what was brought by the years after 1930. It is in this that the topicality and significance of new objectivity now lie.

Magic realism was preceded in the history of visual art by a trend which was inspired by the world of dreams. Magic realism and every other form of experiencing life after the First World War may then also be considered as a reaction against that trend, as a rediscovery of the object through painting, which in the preceding years had remained almost exclusively in the realm of the dream and imagination. On the other hand, however, that trend itself—including surrealism—can also be understood only as a liberation from the oppressed world of small realities, out of which human imagination could not, in the Twenties of our century, escape. The drift towards the realm of dreams is not then an escape from reality, but rather a liberation of human imagination, an attempt to give free rein in painting to the feelings and instincts of man.
This movement in painting has its roots in the works of certain 19th-century poets and writers. Baudelaire and Edgar Allan Poe demanded for creative man the right to give his dreams and fantasies their own form, and *Odilon Redon* **356** was the first person in our age to cross the border between dream and perceptible reality in painting. But a further extension of the human world contributed to the origin of this movement, namely the rise of psychoanalysis and the related discovery of the world of the unconscious. Sigmund Freud's disclosure of the subconscious in man widened the human horizon, and 20th-century art has filled the newly discovered regions with images which belong in them.
The discovery of the realm of dreams and the penetration into the world of fantasy are really principally an extension of reality, or better still a demolishing of the enclosure which restricted perceptible reality narrowly—in fact too narrowly. For dream and reality merge imperceptibly in the realm of fables and fairy tales, in the world of the child. Animals speak, houses fly, and in the midst of normal human life there appear creatures which nobody has ever seen. The freedom of creation and imagination which the child still

graphic art, photography,

architecture and film

131   el lissitzky 1923

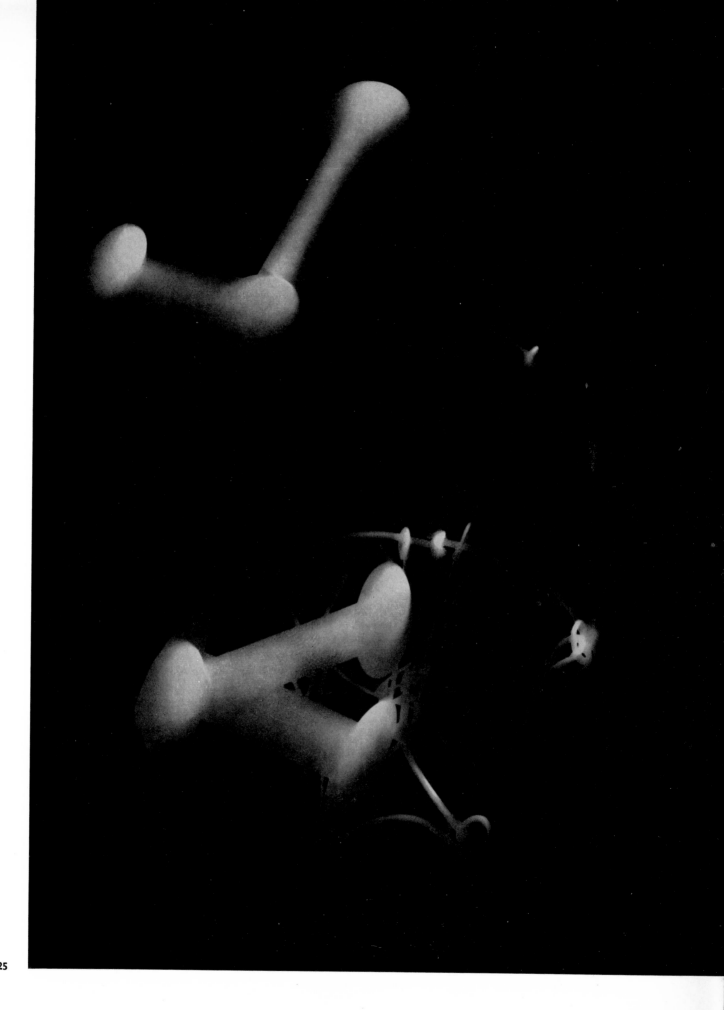

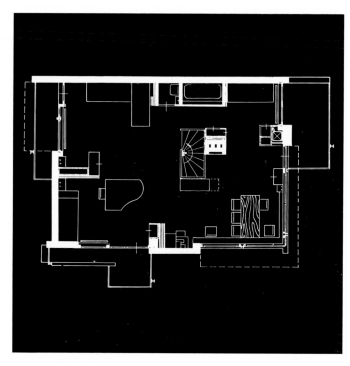

➡

133   g. rietveld 1918

134 g. rietveld en schröder-schräder utrecht 1924

film

135–136 joris ivens 1929–1930

138–140 robert wiene 1919

137 eisenstein potemkin 1925

141 pudowkin 1927

142 victor trivas

143 alexander room 1929

knows, the inspired nature of fantasy which makes animals speak and causes things to become living creatures, were rediscovered by visual art in the years after the First World War.

Chagall is the great master of this movement in painting, and few museums can offer such a richly varied survey of his work as our own, which, thanks to the devotion of P. A. Regnault, has seventeen of his works. Chagall's work combines a child's power of imagination with the mastery of a great painter, the richness of images and symbols of his Jewish faith with the strength and profusion of color from his native Russia. Again and again his works have that moving directness which causes the viewer to feel that they have come straight from a visual and fanciful mind and that they also find a direct path to the viewer's mind, as do fairy tales or fables with their spontaneous appeal.

The museum's collection shows Chagall's work in all its rich nuances and all its variety of creative possibilities. It includes
154 works, such as the *Synagogue at Safad*, which do not appear to differ greatly from a sketchy reproduction of reality, but which on closer inspection show that the color and the brushstroke, which is almost devoid of substance, change this interior of a house of worship into a dream image, into a floating, fanciful space, into a vision. There are other
153 works, such as the *Circus Rider*, which transfer a scene from everyday reality to the realm of the dream and fairy tale by the extreme tenderness of the color, just as much as by the simultaneous presence on the canvas of images taken from reality, memory, and fantasy.
There are other canvases and gouaches, more graceful and lighter in nature, which belong more to the realm of fables.
155 *The Wounded Bird* is one of the most engaging and beautiful works in the collection, and everything in it contributes to giving the feeling of unreality, of transporting everything to a dream world—the color which cannot be brought into relation with any known reality, the space which cannot be circumscribed intellectually, but which is elusive, as in every dream, the figures which stand somewhere, incomprehensibly, in this space—and through all these facts also the object, that puzzling and yet so moving object, of the wounded bird.
Just as this small work transports us through its artistic means to the world of dreams, where we cannot explain anything, but where we willingly accept everything, Chagall's other works bring us, in another way, but by the same means of painting, again and again into another dream.

He is a magician who succeeds in taking us with him to any spot outside everyday reality; to the dream, the fairy tale, the idyl.

There are, however, besides the work of Chagall, other forms of painting which are inspired by dream and fantasy. The work of Paul Klee goes just as far across the border of reality as do the canvases of Chagall. His work also belongs in the world of the elusive. Klee forms images from his dream experiences, from his imagination, images which derive their suggestiveness from the extreme economy of the means
151-152 used, as in his *Composition with Urns*. The watercolor *Bird of Prey* is constructed from a few compelling lines, supported by scanty watercolor tints of extreme fineness. And in his
150 watercolor *The Child with a Blue Hand*, Klee achieves with a few lines and planes of color the definition of a fantastic personage, such as children see and where we, adults, need the work of an artist in order to recall this image in our imagination. Space and time are abolished; in the dream, man can create freely and combine forms into a whole which can certainly exist in the fantasy, but there alone. The combining of things which have nothing to do with one another as far as lucid consciousness is concerned causes a shock to our idea—and this shock evokes new
149 images and dreams. Miró's *Composition with a Shell* works in this way on our subconscious imaginative faculty. Not all art from the realm of dream and fantasy can, however, create a new bond between things so supremely. The dreams of the years after the First World War were often also nightmares. All surrealism lives in this climate of obsession and oppression—yet not an oppression caused by the facts. The suggestive and alarming thing about these works originates precisely from the gruesome absurdity of form
188 and motif. Picasso's etching *Minotaur*, created under the threat of the horrors of the Spanish Civil War, brings the observer into this climate of fear and horror, just as does
215 Max Ernst's painting *The Horde*. The most lucid work in this connection is certainly Lurçat's "Masts and Sails", a cheerless painting of great strength and suggestiveness. Bulging sails flap in the wind on a few heavy masts; they are bulging from its force, but they rise not on a ship, but from the ground—the wind is not driving along a ship but is jerking powerlessly at the masts. Such a symbol—as if taken from a dream—even speaks strongly on its own of despair, of a cheerless feeling of the futile exertion of energy. The feeling of despair is, however, further intensified, elevated, by the faded, grayish-yellow color and by the hurried, shy brushstroke. There thus arises, both through the motif and

VOORBIJTREKKENDE TROEP

Ran   sel
Ran   sel
Ran   sel
Ran-sel
Ran-sel
Ran-sel
Ran-sel
Ran-sel

BLik - ken - trommel
BLik - ken - trommel

BLikken TRommel

RANSEL

BLikken trommel

BLikken trommel

BLikken trommel

RANSEL

(Uit de serie: SOLDATEN 1916)

RUITER

Stap
Paard
STAP
PAARD
Stap
Paard.

STAPPE   PAARD
STAPPE   -PAARD
STAPPE   PAARD
STAPPE PAARD STAPPE PAARD
STEPPE PAARD STEPPE PAARD
STEPPE PAARD STEPPE PAARD
STIPPE PAARD STIPPE PAARD STIPPE PAARD

STIP   PAARD
STIP   PAARD
STIP

WOLK

144   theo van doesburg 1921

1 een proefinstallatie met

50

V. KABEL

2 was op 1 Jan. 1926

+13

UREN in vol bedrijf

3 wij leveren met volle garantie

50

V. KABEL

N.K.F.
DELFT

"H T

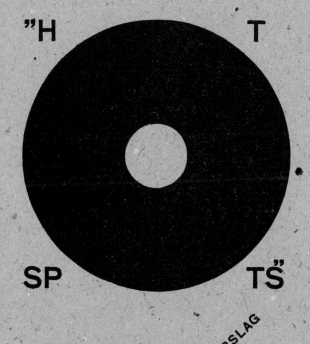

SP TŠ"

"H T SP TŠ leiden onherroepelijk tot den DOORSLAG

Behoedt Uw kabelnet voor "H T SP TŠ door N.K.F. KABEL

146 kurt schwitters 1923

the means of painting, a suggestion of dreariness, a mood
of a perishing world, a nightmare, such as occurred to
many, and in fact to the most sensitive, again and again in
the years after 1918. This is a mood which, with all its
improbability and also its humor, is expressed in Schwitters'
collages, being combinations of refuse, old streetcar tickets,
etc., which the artist reconciles with one another.

177

The historical situation today has certainly altered very
much compared to that after the First World War, and yet
the art of those postwar years, which rediscovered the
dream world, is still of great importance to us. There was,
of course, much in surrealism which had merely an
accidental connection with visual art. The important works
of this school nevertheless extended mankind's horizon,
they reallocated to fantasy its own place, and created an
art which, in spite of its use of the forms of visible reality,
can neither be approached nor influenced by photography.
The work of Chagall and Klee, but just as much that of
Lurçat and Max Ernst, has opened up for art extended
domains of the human mind, and has again made painting
receptive to a form of inspiration which can proceed from
the inner life of man himself, and not from the world
outside him.

The language of this painting is so suggestive and of such
great influence on contemporary artists because its form,
its symbols, and its atmosphere come from that realm of
the unconscious, which is equally familiar, and at the same
time foreign, to us all. Here modern art has succeeded
again in creating a valid language of signs and symbols, a
language which we do not always like to hear today, merely
because it reminds us of the despair of former days.
Nevertheless, in the works in which fear and oppression
do not constitute a starting point for the creation, for
example in those of Chagall, contemporary art has again
found a source of inspiration which—precisely through
its generality and suprapersonal character—will contribute
much towards deepening art. The colors and forms from
the world of dreams still live, while the technique and
fortuitous situation of surrealism already belong to the past.
The world of the dream and the world of things—those
were the discoveries in painting in the years after the
First World War. The discovery which preceded them
opened up another field and its consequences have been felt
everywhere since. The painters of the years around 1920
rediscovered painting itself. Although these discoveries
took place in all parts of the world more or less at the same
time, the Netherlands nevertheless made an important

and fundamental contribution to the growth of present-day
art in this field.

The somewhat obscure name of "abstract art" is used for
the works which were created during or shortly after the
First World War and which were at that time the newest
and most daring in the field of visual art. What does this
attempt, in those days so revolutionary, at a revision of
values mean; what did it mean then, and what does it mean
today? From the start it was, for the artists who formed
this new movement, a matter of creating an absolute art of
painting, consequently an art which was completely
autonomous as regards its sister arts and which rejected all
influences from the outside, desiring to find its power of
expression solely through its own means. In their effort to
keep painting pure, artists such as Kandinsky, Malevich,
and Mondriaan went so far that they completely banished
the subject, the visible motif as the starting point of the
painting. They wanted their art to be absolute and
autonomous, like music. Just as the musician creates works
by means of sound and rhythm, that is, exclusively with
musical means, the painters of this generation wanted to
create works which had arisen solely from the means of
painting. Color and line were consequently to play in their
work the part of sound and rhythm in music. This
revolutionary change in painting certainly resulted from the
structure and events of the period. At that time there was
a violent reaction by artists against naturalistic art. A
representation of nature was denied any artistic validity,
since technical equipment, i.e., photography, was itself in
a position to record the image of nature. Perceptible reality
as a subject, as a motif for visual art, consequently became
unacceptable. There was, however, at that time also no
spiritual reality, such as the chronicle and doctrine of the
Holy Scriptures or the stories and allegories of ancient
times, which was sufficiently valid to be accepted as a
subject for modern painting. And people were then
seeking, in the years of the First World War, precisely a
content which was universal, now that they were becoming
aware of the necessity for a general lawfulness, a language
and a message, which surpassed the limitation of the
individual. Abstract art is, in many respects, a reaction
against the extreme individualism of an earlier period, a
reaction against the idolization of one's own personality
and feelings. In abstract art the means of painting did in
fact become the carriers of the artistic creation—a new
visual language was formed by the painters of this
generation.

painting and sculpture

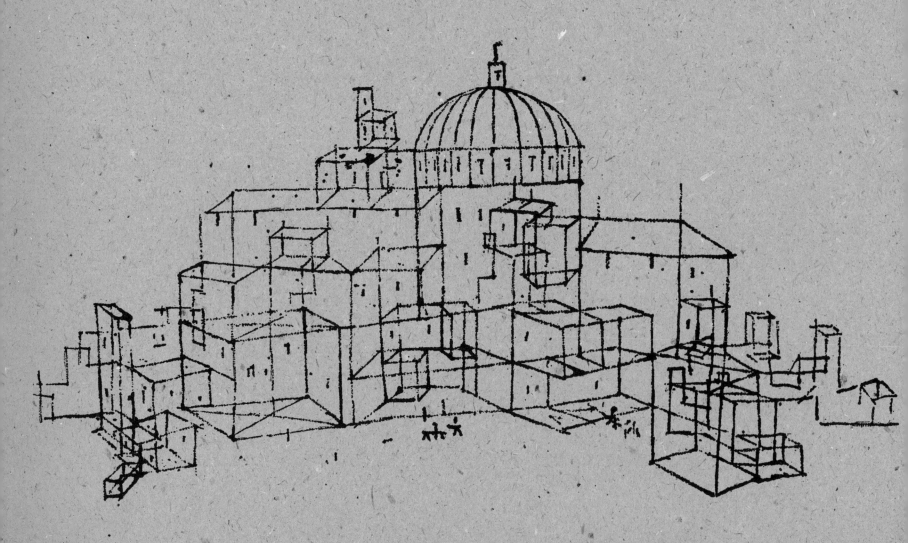

147 paul klee 1929

148   henri laurens 1919

149   joan mirò 1931

150   1939

paul klee

151   1938

153   marc chagall 1931

154   marc chagall 1931

155   marc chagall 1935

156　raoul dufy 1938

157　massimo campigli 1935

158   massimo campigli

The strictest and most consistent form of this abstract art arose in the Netherlands. "De Stijl" (The Style) is Holland's essential contribution to modern art. The efforts of the painters of De Stijl—Mondriaan, van Doesburg, van der Leck—were directed towards expressing in a generally valid language what has always been the essence of art, namely harmony and equilibrium. They felt that this harmony, the mutual abolition of antitheses, not only constituted the essence of art, but was the basic reason for everything that exists. Consequently, because they sought the universally applicable law of art and the world, neither the subject content nor indeed even any accidental motif of the painter could any longer find a place in their paintings. Their works show also the most extreme economy. These painters use exclusively the elements of *painting*, i.e., the straight line, the right angle and the three primary colors red, yellow, and blue, supplemented by the primary noncolors white and black. With this economical arsenal of means they none the less succeeded in constructing a world in which the feeling of arrangement and harmony predominated to such an extent that they thought they had banned all tragedy, and with it all individual unrest, from the art of their time.

The art of De Stijl is preeminently Dutch in character, although its efforts were directed towards universal values. The Dutch puritanism, which has become a feature of our people, is reflected in the works of Mondriaan, van Doesburg and van der Leck. It is the same puritanism which in the 16th century banned paintings from the churches out of respect for the absoluteness of what was sacred, desiring in our century—in the spirit of iconoclasm—to ban every motif, every nongeometrical form, and every mixed color from art.

The art of De Stijl fits in, however, not only with the Dutch spiritual tradition, but also with the country and the world of that time. The Netherlands inspired the art of De Stijl because the whole country had been built and arranged by man. It is the mind and hand of man which has given the Dutch landscape its character, its "style". We therefore find in the Netherlands again and again the straight line, the right angle, the square, which are predominantly forms of the human mind and not of nature. And it seems in no way accidental that the founding of De Stijl—of the group as well as the journal—in 1917 almost coincided with one of the greatest victories of the Netherlands over nature, namely the plan for reclaiming the Zuider Zee. In the work of De Stijl the will of man to dominate nature acquired form—a will which has always been present in the Nether-

lands and which was revived principally at the beginning of this century.

De Stijl was, from the start, strongly linked to architecture, which was acquainted with the suprapersonal concept of style even more than were the sister arts. The influence of this type of painting on architecture and the applied arts is therefore obvious. Van Doesburg himself drew plans for his house and in this and other buildings applied color in combination with architecture. Rietveld, who linked up with the group quite early, designed furniture in the very first years of De Stijl in which the movement's elementary principles are also revealed. Rietveld's *House in Utrecht*, dated 1923-24, of which the museum has plans and the model, is a monument of the spirit of abstract art converted into the language of architecture. Oud's designs for sections of Rotterdam are an expression of the same attempt, and van der Leck's color work in the Government Aeronautical School at Eelde (of which the museum has a model) shows how architecture and painting are dominated by the same spirit of clarity and precision. The rise of abstract art, especially its Dutch branch De Stijl, is today still of great importance, and not merely because this movement purified art of numerous incidentals which threatened to choke its language. The great act of abstract art is that it again caused painting to consider its elements, its own means, that it has, as it were, for the first time rewritten a grammar for the language of painting.

Its Dutch branch, De Stijl, again molded the feeling for purity, tidiness, and order, in which the Netherlands may at present also be considered exemplary.

Abstract art, and particularly its Dutch from, was, with surrealism, the most important trend formed after the First World War. Yet in the polyphony of voices which dominated European art between the two wars other sounds were also to be heard—melodies which had already begun before the war, but which had not yet everywhere reached their climax, their full musical development. "Expressionism" as well as "cubism" had begun in the heroic years between 1907 and 1914, but they had by no means yet penetrated into all countries—for example, into the Netherlands.

It was fairly late that expressionism, which had its origin in the Netherlands—with Vincent van Gogh—was again accepted in that country. In 1917, the same year in which De Stijl started, there was founded in Groningen in the north a society called "De Ploeg" (The Plow), which

159   jan sluyters 1924

160

162

161

160   frits van den berghe 1928
161   frits van den berghe ±1937
162   constant permeke ±1936
163   constant permeke ± 1930

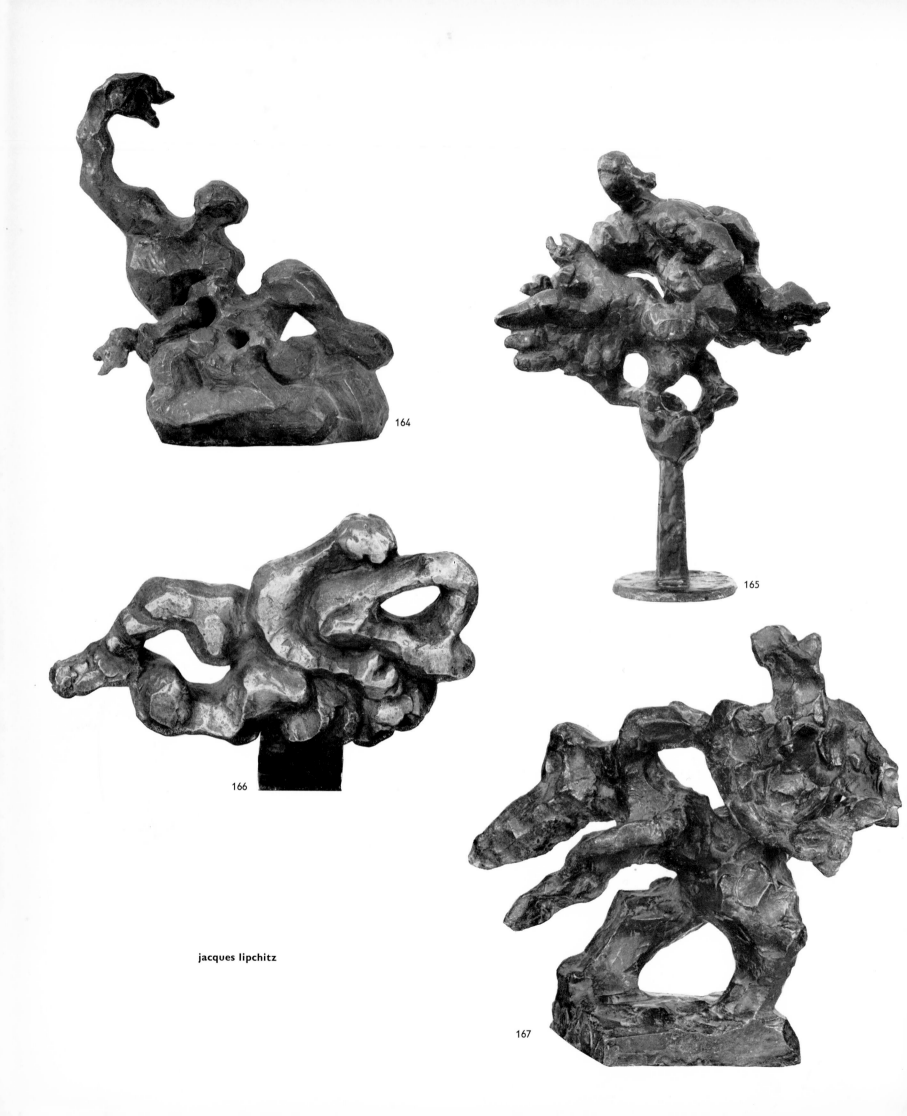

164

165

166

jacques lipchitz

167

168   otto dix 1923–'24

169   max beckmann 1921

170   max beckmann 1939

171   georges rouault 1926

172 chaïm soutine 1926

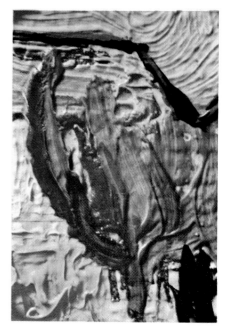

174

173   jan wiegers 1924
174   van gogh détail 1888
175   heinrich campendonk 1918
176   herman kruyder ±1933

175

176

178

179

werkman

177   kurt schwitters 1927
178   h. n. werkman 1941
179   h. n. werkman 1942

werkman

180 ±1927

werkman

181   ± 1924

OO
M
M
M
M
M
M

OOOO
MM
MM
MM
MM

LENIN

184 léger 1919   185 julio gonzalez 1936

186   antoine pevsner 1937

187   ossip zadkine 1939

188   pablo picasso 1935

embraced the expressionist painters of the north. German expressionism was the main influence, in both the vivid coloring and the terse composition. Jan Wiegers emerges as the strongest personality in this group. His *Landscape with*

173 *Red Trees* is a striking example of this northern expressionism. The fierce red trees which flare up like flames show how much the spirit of dynamics predominates in expressionist creation, just as the verb acquires a new, major importance in contemporary poetry.

Jan Sluyters had worked in Amsterdam in the expressionist style as early as 1907, principally under the influence of the French expressionists, the *Fauves*. His later work, particularly after the Staphorst period, is typical of Dutch expressionism—somber in color and with a strong

159 expressive power. His *Self-portrait*, dating from 1924, is a characteristic example of this powerful and brutal method of painting. Sluyters' later work became milder in mood, a certain peacefulness predominating; nevertheless there still resided in it the violence of the painter of the self-portrait of 1924. Chabot's paintings, but also his *Zealand*

204 *Peasant*, hewn from a millstone, breathe this same atmosphere.

Finally, Kruyder is also one of the masters of Dutch expressionism. In all his works he sought the elementary simplicity and primitive passions of life. His small sculpture

203 *The Peasant* is an early example of his style in which a primitive force attempts to find expression, and his later work was pervaded by a vivid vitality in the color and

176 drawing. *The Cock* is no longer a representation of any animal: the work has become a symbol of the impulse to live and of a primordial strength, an expression of the elementary stirrings of life. This expression of invisible forces lurking behind reality is typical of expressionism and is likewise characteristic of the new attitude to life which prevailed, not only in the Netherlands, but also in the whole of Europe for a short period at the beginning of the 20th century.

The same attitude to life and reality can be discerned most clearly at this time in Belgium. The work of the Belgian

160-163 expressionists—*Permeke* and *Frits van den Berghe*—is in fact contemporary with that of Dutch expressionism, and is based on the same experiences, namely the crisis of certainties. In France too the same tragic attitude to life

171 forced its way through. *Rouault's Clown* and *Soutine's*

172 *Slaughtered Ox* are striking examples of it, and only here

156 and there, as in *Dufy's* work—represented here by his *Regatta*

—does the expressionism of the École de Paris acquire the character of a happy, seething ecstasy. In sculpture—

164 particularly in the work of *Lipchitz*— the relationship with the tragic obsession of Soutine and Rouault is obvious. Germany was the country of origin of expressionism. Here young artists revolted for the first time against the strict, impersonal nature of rules and laws, against convention and

170 its artistic counterpart, academicism. *Beckmann's Double Portrait*, painted in Amsterdam during his exile, is still a reflection of this first revolt, evoked by the horrors of a new and even more barbaric rule which caused the individual to stand even more isolated and on his own.

175 *Campendonk's Man with a Flower*, one of the masterpieces of German expressionism, shows the linking of this with the discoveries of cubism. Expressionism had surrendered to the ecstatic power of passion. Cubism sought its reason for existence in the strict, architectonic construction of a visual grammar, a counterpoint. Only seldom are the two opposing movements at work at the same time. Their linkage stamps Campendonk's paintings—as well as some of the works of "Der Blaue Reiter" (The Blue Rider)—as exceptional masterpieces, in which ecstasy and control balance one another.

The cool, ascetic movement of cubism still produced many a masterpiece after the First World War, although its heroic period was prior to 1914. The museum has a few

191 examples, such as Picasso's *Still Life with a Guitar,*

192 Braque's *Still Life with Fruit*, and in particular Léger's

193 *Three Comrades*, a work which embodies fully the clarity and strict construction of cubism. The two sculptures by

148-187 *Henri Laurens*, as well as *Zadkine's Torso*, also show clearly the rigorous methodology which is the main theme of cubist work, namely, the construction of a work of art according to the laws of a visual grammar, which isolates the planes, reduces the syntax of the forms to the forces which determine the optical image and its effect. A plastic work which breathes this spirit is Pevsner's

186 *Construction for an Airfield*. Here the inspiration comes, not from a visual impression, but from the technical world of forms and mathematics, but it is just as much the contrapuntal elaboration which makes it such an exceptional work. This strict mathematical composition is characteristic of a whole branch of abstract art, the branch which desires to exclude the individual arbitrariness and fortuity of the artist for the sake of a language which is general and transcends the individual element.

The works of some artists who moved less far from visible

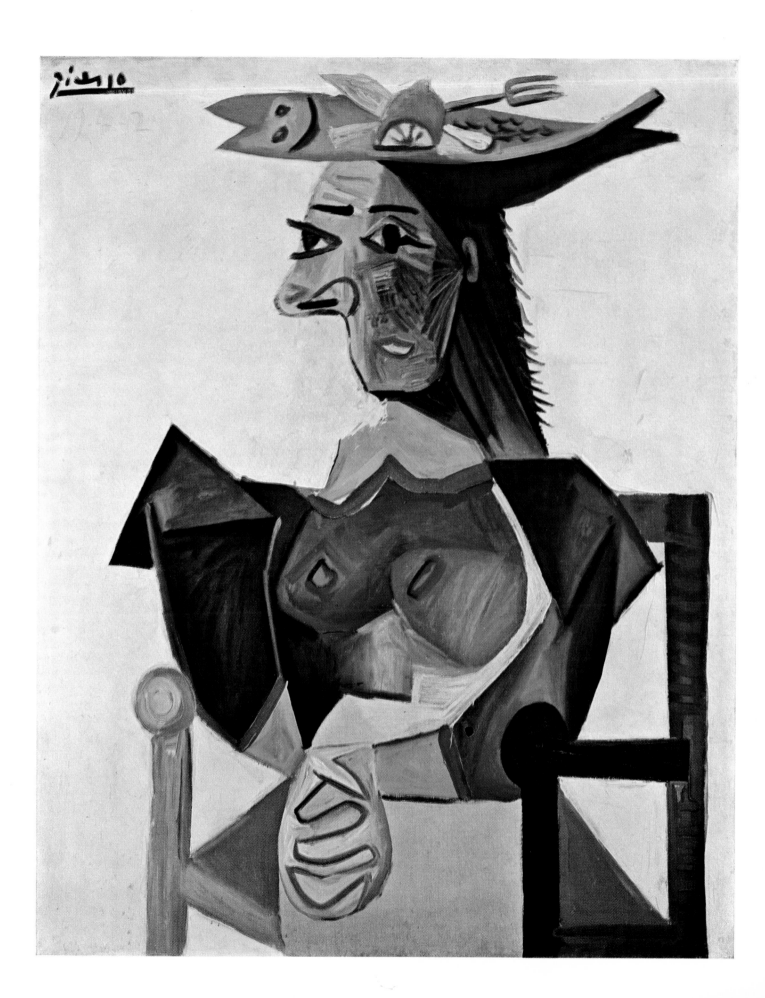

191   pablo picasso 1924

192   georges braque 1932

193   fernand léger 1920

191

192

194

195

196

197

de stijl

198   charley toorop 1932

holland

peter alma ±1924

199

200

201

202 jan wiegers 1930

203   herman kruyder 1932   204   hendrik chabot 1933 ⬆

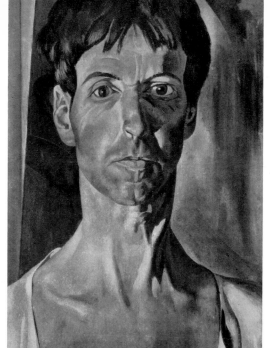

205

208

206

209

207

211a

211b

211

210

205   stanley spencer 1936
206   dick ket 1931
207   charley toorop 1938
208   raoul hynckes 1928
209   w. schuhmacher 1929
210   a. c. willink 1926
211   a. c. willink 1932
211a   johan polet 1919
211b   h. m. werelaar 1934

212　dick ket 19

3   max ernst 1926

214   john raedecker 1920

215   max ernst 1927

216   oskar schlemmer 1931

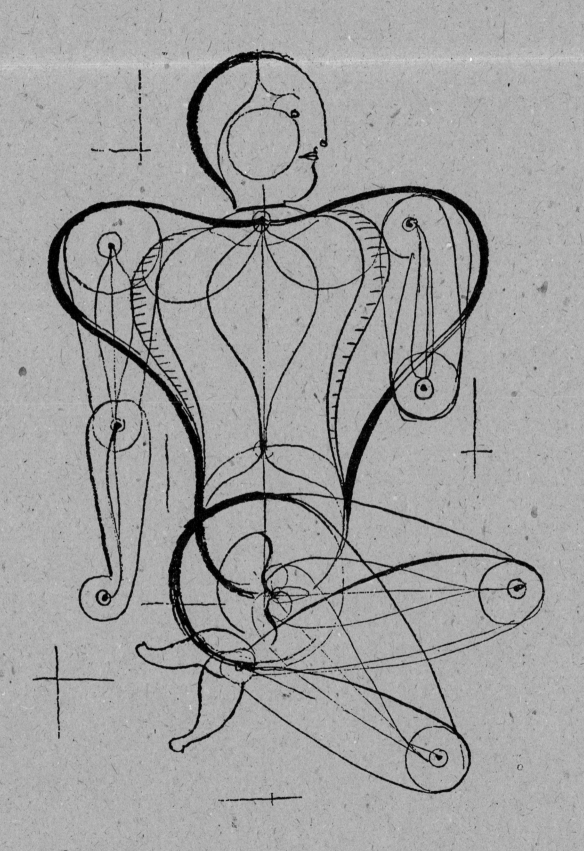

217 oskar schlemmer 1919

reality can likewise also not withdraw from the influence

157 of this powerful discipline. *Campigli*'s *Women on the Beach*

185 and *Gonzales*'s sculpture *La Montserrat* derive their monumentality, their closed construction, from the schooling
of cubism and its strict methodical simplification. The
strict spiritual discipline of cubism—the spirit of mathematics and architecture—was of decisive influence on the center
of German art after the First World War, the "Bauhaus"

216 (Design Center). *Schlemmer*'s *Large Head and Model* is
an example of this ascetic discipline, which in Germany
formed the direct opposite of ecstatic expressionism.
Modern functional architecture arose in the field of
influence of the Bauhaus, and "constructivist" sculpture
shows a relationship to it. The separate movements in
visual art moved along side by side in the period between
the two wars like parts in a great symphonic score;
together they formed the richness and variety of this
epoch. Only few individuals succeeded in combining various

175 movements in their work, in their personality. *Campendonk*
synthesized expressionism and cubism at the beginning of
the period in 1918. In the years just before the Second

178 World War the Dutchman *Werkman* succeeded in combining
with a personal style in his printing all the acquisitions of
this period—the strict construction of cubism, the colorful
passion of the expressionists, the dream world of the
discoverers of the realm between reality and vision. His
work opened new paths for the graphic arts, particularly as
regards the use of color. Through its very personal
character it summarized the acquisitions of the period
between the two wars into a synthesis both in the
Netherlands and later also elsewhere.

221   marc chagall 1922

'17-'07

c the turning point

film and sculpture

223

230

224

226

231

227

232

225

228

233

229

234

film

235   wilhelm lehmbruck 1913

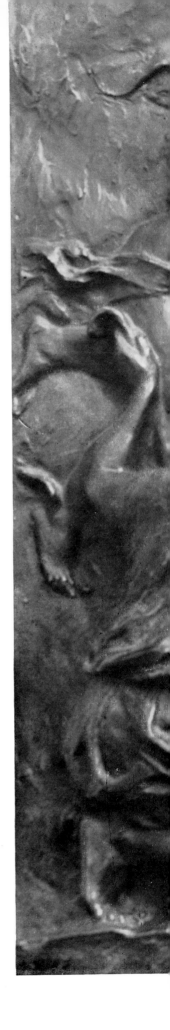

238   e. a. bourdelle ±1910

239   1909 rik wouters   240   1913

c the turning point

The years prior to the First World War have sometimes
been called the heroic period of new art. The great voyages
of discovery in these years extended our horizon. Cubism
and expressionism opened perspectives for much that was
to develop later.

Cubism occupies a relatively small place in our collection,
yet this movement has been of great importance in 20th
century painting, and a great number of later works would
have been impossible without the experiments of the small
group which founded the movement. Mondriaan's abstract
imagery resulted from it, and the whole of the École de
Paris continued to build on the findings of Picasso and
Braque after 1908 which formed its basis. Nevertheless this
movement, which was so important in European art, never
found much response in the Netherlands. *Sluyters*   314
experimented a few times in his early works with the
language of cubist forms; *Leo Gestel* is the only Dutch   316
painter on whose work this movement left anything
approaching a permanent impression.

The name "cubism" was—as often happens in the history of
art—used originally by a derisive critic who wished to point
to the blocklike structure of these paintings. He nevertheless
hit upon one of the essential features of this movement,
which was based on the art of Cézanne and his statement
that every natural form could be reduced to a sphere, cone,
or cylinder. Coupled with this tendency on the part of the
first cubists to rediscover a geometrical structure, there
was also the strong impression of southern French nature,
where geometrical forms appear so clearly, together with
the Latin need of the cubists for a clear, transparent, and
balanced structure in their work.

Our museum has only a few works from the so-called heroic
period of cubism, that is to say, the period in which Picasso
and Braque were mastering the movement's formal
language and syntax, namely Braque's *Still Life with Jug and*   256
Bottles, and Léger's gouache *Smoke*. From these early   258
works, dating from prior to 1914, it appears that the
stereometric structure is certainly not the only acquisition
of cubism. Besides the mastering of a geometrical basis,
there is equally a new concept of space which breaks with
the laws of linear perspective. From the time of the
Renaissance up to cubism, space in painting had been
constructed from a fixed point of observation, and each
object within that space had been subordinated to that one
point. The new cubist view of space, on the other hand,
takes the objects themselves as the starting point. The
painter, and with him the viewer, moves around the object

painting

241   claude monet ±1915

242 pierre bonnard 1917

244   gino severini 1914

cubisme   245   piet mondriaan 1914

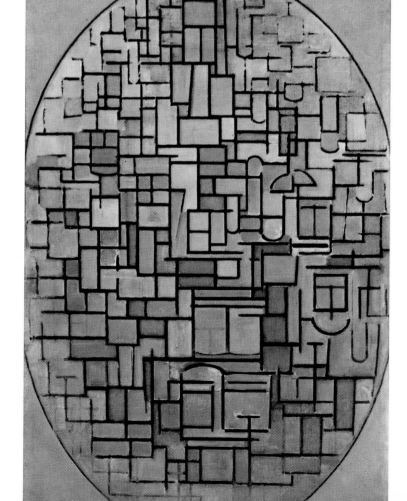

246 piet mondriaan 1913

suprematisme   **247**   kasimir malewitch ±1914

248   kasimir malewitch ±1912

249   kasimir malewitch ±1911

250 kasimir malewitch ±1911

252   marc chagall 1912–1913

253 1913 wassily kandinsky   254 1910

255 robert delaunay 1912–1913

cubisme   ⬆ 256   georges braque 1909   257   van gogh 1885 ➡

and views it from the front, side, back, from above and below. Thus, on the one hand, movement, a characteristic feature of our century, is integrated in the paintings of this period, while on the other hand the view of things is released from the all too static and individual tradition of a fixed point of observation. These innovations characterize clearly the revolutionary nature of cubism—a completely new relationship between the painter and his material seems to have arisen. The objects acquire a new strength in their portrayal, a firm structure and a powerful volume. They are, however, at the same time split into their various facets, which again contribute towards elucidating clearly the structure of the object.

281 The same laws apply in sculpture. *Duchamp-Villon's Horse* shows how the artist reduces forms to geometrical elements and how he constructs an image from them which radiates energy, movement, and tension. This results in a form which is so much a concentration of strength that the observer will think of an engine or a machine—the machine which had, in fact, been such a prominent source of inspiration for the cubists, since they constructed their paintings and images from parts of objects, using the same precision as those with which the constructor of machines works.

This same technique of constructing a space from the sections of objects was applied in the paintings in our collection.

244 *Severini's Train for the Wounded* also creates, through the juxtaposition of various phases and facets of objects, a suggestion of intensive and rhythmic movement. Many painters of the École de Paris came from cubism, but Fernand Léger remained most faithful to the spirit of this movement. His art is, even more than that of the other cubists, inspired by technical matters, the machine and its degree of precision, and the clearness of technical shaping is vividly expressed in his work, intensified by a bright, radiant coloring.

The influence of cubism extended even further. Chagall, the master of the realm of dreams, was also deeply affected by the new concept of space. Three paintings from his early period in our collection bear witness to this influence,

251 namely, the large painting *Pregnant Woman*, the other large
252 canvas *The Violinist*, and finally the *Self-Portrait*. In all these three works Chagall brings together on the canvas pieces of reality which cannot be perceived simultaneously, and makes them flow into one another. Thus he frees painting of the fixed conventions of space and time,

conventions which have just as little validity in dreams as in his paintings. The world of dreams, of the imagination, is here more highly pictorial and inspiring than perceptible reality—the painter draws on his dreams for his work. The means for making this dream world visible in his paintings were, however, suggested to him by cubism. Its influence can consequently lead to an expression of the dream world; it can, however, also lead straight to an abstract formulation.

Delaunay's composition *Revolving Forms*, dating from **255** 1912-13, stands alongside Chagall's works. Delaunay starts from a similar, optical theme—the view from his window—and he varies it in the manner of a musical theme: diminutions, repetitions, and stretti lie side by side and penetrate one another, so that a unity is formed of visual melodies, a sort of optical counterpoint, in which the original material is completely lost. It is not the motif which constitutes the work of art, but its musical development. The formality of the composition, the method of this musical development, come straight from cubism.

The development of cubism towards abstract art—corresponding to the growth of Mondriaan's and van Doesburg's art—can be seen most clearly from the work of the Russian Malevich, the museum having a comprehensive collection of his *canvases*. After his early cubist paintings, e.g., the **261-279** "cubist rose," which are constructed entirely according to the method of the French cubists, with a little blue and brown and by means of a series of planes which create the space, his shaping becomes more and more attached to the plane as time goes on. His composition *The Guardsman* **248** is an example of this flat style, in which color contrasts again play a more important part. In his effort to make his work purer and purer and more independent of the fortuities of perceptible reality, he arrives at a complete rejection of the world of perceptible forms and a restriction to simple geometrical forms. His "suprematist" style began in 1913 as the first conquest of an abstract language of forms from the field of geometry—a fact to which the development of cubism had given rise. His series of suprematist works shows what richness of compositions and expression of feelings an art is capable of when it restricts itself to the use of geometrical forms, without reverting to associations with perceived reality.

This same development from cubism to abstract art started later in the Netherlands, namely, in the work of Mondriaan and van Doesburg. The most typical work of Dutch cubism in our Collection is Gestel's *Figure of a Woman*, a painting **316** which can with honor represent the cubist movement by its consistent geometrical shaping and its coloring restrained

313 for the sake of the form. The work links up with the style of the French painter *le Fauconnier*, who brought cubism from France to the Netherlands where he exerted a deep influence on a number of artists.

Simultaneously with cubism in France, there arose in Italy a movement in painting which was inspired chiefly by speed and dynamics, namely "futurism". The museum has a single, but exceedingly typical, example of this movement, to wit, 282 *Balla's Racing Car, Abstract Speed*. Here the movement is split into its facets, in the same way as objects are in cubism. Through this succession of moments on the same canvas a compelling suggestion of speed is produced. Time and space, the two basic problems of our time, thus also again became a problem for 20th-century painting, and the foundation for their solution was laid by cubism and futurism.

At the beginning of our century, in the years around 1907, a style of visual art known as "expressionism" dominated Europe for a short time. During a brief period it gave expression to the spiritual life of our continent. All nations contributed to it, and a revolutionary spirit, which created a new view on reality and human life, began to find a suitable language in this new style of painting in about 1905.

That was preeminently a revolutionary year—the year of the outbreak of the first Russian revolution also caused rebellious forces to break loose elsewhere. This revolt was directed not only against an antiquated social policy, but principally against an obsolete and disintegrated view of reality. The painters of the 19th century, and with them the whole of society at that time, had accepted reality as an established fact, as a reality in which a priori nothing could be changed. They tried to express that reality objectively, in a way which agreed with the scientific data of their time. Protest against this reality, against these facts, had scarcely been heard at all prior to 1905. Vincent van Gogh was the only person in the 19th century who, not being satisfied with the existing order, sought further behind its appearance, the only person who endeavored to remodel and change reality so that his image might become "truer than the literal truth".

By about 1905 faith in society, in the 19th-century slogans of progress, civilization, and Western culture, had fallen so low that a new attitude towards reality became possible. It was at that time no longer a question of accepting reality, but of changing and improving it.

In the world of painting this new attitude acquired form in expressionism. The painters of a new generation no longer adopted merely a passive and registering attitude towards reality—they wanted to take an active part in building a new world.

The perceptible world was for the young expressionist painters of that time no longer a fact, but always a new problem which was seeking a solution. The role of the subject, of the motif, therefore also changes. It is no longer a static fact which is described, but a struggle of forces which has to be resolved by the painter. With the year 1905 the center of gravity of European painting moves from describing existing data toward a new form of dynamics, towards a stirring of the painter himself. The movings of the human soul acquire more importance than the facts of the external world, and human passions dominate scientific order. Expressionism is the revolt of a passionate, romantic youth against a static view of life. It is, as van Gogh wrote of Delacroix, "le renouvellement de la passion."

The effort to interpret a deep human passion, and through this passion, to give the face of reality a different aspect, is revealed both in the composition and in the feeling for color of the expressionists. They no longer seek the refined play of lines of their predecessors—their lines and planes strike against one another heavily and dramatically. Harmony is here no longer the aim, but a passionate drama. The generation of 1905 sees the world no longer as a system of facts, but as a struggle of forces, forces of elemental and magical violence. It is therefore also understandable that early expressionism found a source of inspiration in the art of the primitive races, whose world is likewise dominated by elemental forces and whose world of forms has a dramatic quality, such as that sought by expressionism. As far as colors are concerned, the strong, vived hues and their contrast predominate—gradations disappear more and more. Color and form now have a new purpose. It is no longer to describe an object, but to transfer an emotion, a passion, to the observer. Van Gogh, the father of expressionism, had already written: "If one were to make the color correct or the drawing quite exact, one would not be able to convey these emotions." Color as well as drawing become for expressionism a means for interpreting simple, elementary passions, and the subject of the painting becomes, together with the color and form, the bearer of this human desire for expression, for voicing feelings.

258   léger 1913

261

262

263

264

cubisme

267

268

269

27●

expressionisme + fauvisme

274

275

suprematisme

malewitch

265   266

271   272   273

276   277   278   279

280 ± 1913 r. duchamp-villon 281 1914 ➡

futurisme ⬆ 282 giacomo balla 1913 283 umberto boccioni 1912

284 kirchner ±1910

285 schmidt-rottluff 1917

Expressionism has in this connection often been accused of having coarsened and barbarized the traditional world of forms. This barbarization nevertheless had a purpose and a meaning, namely, through an aversion to refinement and through a simplification of language and content to revert to an art which would interpret the social attitude to life of an age and of a community, which would be wider than the small circles of art lovers and esthetes.

The museum has a varied collection of expressionist works, among the earlier being *Kirchner*'s *Women in a Landscape*, his figure painting *Fränzi*, and *Schmidt-Rottluff*'s *Landscape at Dangast*. We are struck in these works by the vividness of the color and at the same time by the simplified, summarizing form, which is also characteristic of Kirchner's and Schmidt-Rottluff's *sculptures* and of the graphic arts in German expressionism. From about the same period comes *Kokoschka*'s *Portrait of William Wauer*, in which the color does not shine, but merely develops a somber glow. Kokoschka's portrait is likewise not intended as a likeness, but merely wishes to express a state of mind of nervous torment, such as was then typical of the spiritual attitude of many people. The person portrayed provided him with the occasion for it. The colors in the portrait have the same nervous quivering as the hands and the face of the model. They resemble the result of a fermentation—that same fermentation which is really the subject of this portrait. Expressionism did not in all cases express the tragic nature of its own time in such a vivid and poignant manner. There are other works, in which the realization of the tragic situation prior to the First World War and just after it is tempered by a lyrical feeling to a suggestion of *Weltschmerz*. *Marc*'s *Horses*, *Jawlensky*'s *Woman's Head* and *Lehmbruck*'s *Woman's Face* are examples of this style in which—and this is not accidental—a woman is often the subject, in other words, the bearer of the emotions. There is also a path which leads from expressionism to abstract art, just as there was one from cubism. The need to turn away from the fortuitous forms of perceived reality and to express in an abstract language the invisible values of reality then dominated artists of all trends. Kandinsky was the pioneer on this path. His painting *Houses at Murnau*, dating from 1909, shows a vividness of colors and brushstroke similar to Kirchner's work of the preceding years. Yet in about 1910 Kandinsky had, in a few watercolors, created the first abstract works by divesting the areas of vivid color and the leaping lines of his expressionist paintings of their importance as regards perceptible reality. The "mood" of

his paintings, their musical tempo and their key, nevertheless remained the same: a sparkling, vivid rhythm characterizes Kandinsky's early works, such as the painting *The East*, dating from 1913, in our collection. Later his "compositions" —as he calls his works through a conscious association with music—become calmer. The background and forms become more separated, but the richness of forms, the capriciousness and liveliness of the discoveries, remain. His paintings suggest the magnificence and colorful luxury of folk art, the richness of motifs which we know from the embroideries of his native Russia. This one source of abstract art does not belie his Eastern origin, and the richness of forms, the vividness of color, the violence of emotions, come straight from expressionism.

What then is the importance of expressionism for contemporary art? That importance lies principally in the fact that expressionism cleared the path for modern art. It was the first of the modern movements which turned resolutely from the representation of perceptible reality. Expressionism accustomed artists and the public to accepting those "developments, deviations, changes in reality" (van Gogh), as a result of which alone could human feelings be expressed. The most important gain from expressionism for contemporary art is, however, probably the fact that the artists of the expressionist generation again laid stress on human imagination, the gift of man for expressing his feelings. They were the first who again confronted nature actively and freely and in this way broke through the tradition which assigned to the painter the task of a more passive, recording attitude with regard to reality.

Expressionism is of importance for modern art principally because of this new attitude which prefers inspiration to the representation of nature. The richly varied world of art in the years shortly before the First World War nevertheless becomes even more fascinating because of the fact that, besides the innovators of a young generation —cubists and expressionists—older artists were at the same time at work, who had in their youth also been innovators: the survivors of the impressionist generation.

Renoir, one of the pioneers of impressionism, had in these years, because of severe physical suffering, been forced to say farewell to painting. He had, however, succeeded in expressing his message of happiness and joy in living in his *sculptures*. A younger master, following in his footsteps—the Belgian Rik Wouters—interpreted this same joy of living in his *figures* and *paintings*.

The activity of this older generation nevertheless appears

expressionism

proportion

288

291

289

290

292

293   e. l. kirchner ±1908

294   edgar tytgat

295 e. l. kirchner 1913

296

297

298

299

expressionism

otto müller

300   1920

303   ±1915

304   ±1915

305   ±1914

ernst ludwig kirchner

308

309

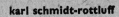
karl schmidt-rottluff

301 1914

302 1914

306 ± 1914

jacoba van heemskerck

307 ± 1914

241 particularly absorbing also because a path seems to lead
from impressionism to abstract shaping. *Claude Monet's*
later work *The Garden at Giverny* does not describe a piece
of nature, but takes this piece of reality merely as a reason
for a stirring, flashing projection which has little relationship
with its starting point in reality. Here again we see how
all generations in an epoch—however different their origin,
education and language may be—are confronted by one
problem, this problem being in those years the abstract
interpretation of reality. Thus through the pioneering
spirit of those days, Monet's painting—alongside the works
painted by Malevich, Kandinsky and Delaunay in the same
period—can have for us today in the 1960's an inspiring
contemporaneity.

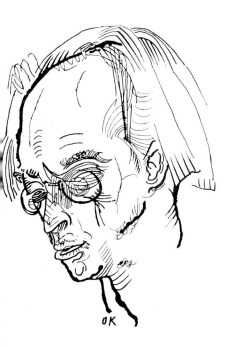

310 oskar kokoschka 1909

312 egon schiele 1914

311 oskar kokoschka 1910

313

314

315

316

317 kees van dongen 1910 ➡

'07-'70

d around van gogh

318   auguste rodin 1884   photo stedelijk 1960

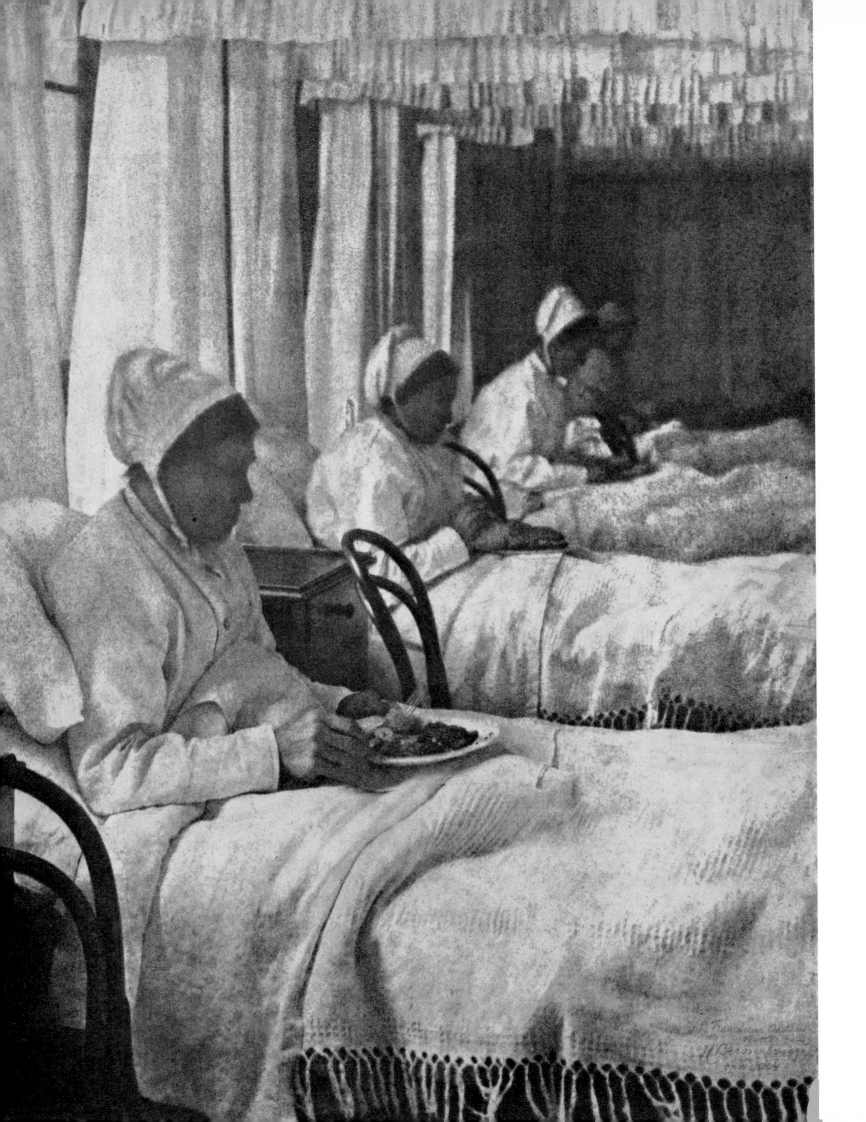

319   h. berssenbrugge 1904   320   j. goedeljee

photo 1900

322 stedelijk detail

321 a. w. weissman stedelijk museum 1895

325   326   327   328   329

324 detail

323 h. p. berlage 1897–1903

330

331

325 th. nieuwenhuis 1905

326 g. w. dijsselhof ± 1899

327 k. p. c. de bazel

328 k. p. c. de bazel

329 ± 1905

330 h. p. berlage ± 1909

331 h. p. berlage ± 1909

332 ± 1870

332

333-334   amsterdam 1900

336-337   méliès 1901

335   lumière 1895

film 1900

d around van gogh

The first years of the new century saw the birth of a new, revolutionary art, an art which had broken with perception and reality and which operated according to its own procedure and the laws of the human heart and reason. In the same years there developed and flourished alongside expressionism an art which did not, it is true, carry out the revolutionary break with reality, but at the same time cannot be said to have played a conservative role. This was an art in which that seeking and groping typical of the new century found its expression.

The first years of the 20th century are rendered extremely complicated for the contemporary observer by the simultaneous existence of a number of intersecting movements in visual art. At the beginning of the century the impressionists Monet, Degas, and Renoir were living in France alongside the great innovator Cézanne, and at the same time there were working young modernists such as Picasso, Rouault, and Vlaminck, as well as painters who had not broken completely with tradition, such as Bonnard, Vuillard, and Matisse. In sculpture Rodin stood alongside Maillol. This picture is to be seen in all countries. In Germany, for example, at the same time as the old Menzel we find an already established generation—of Liebermann and Corinth—standing alongside the young expressionists Kirchner, Nolde, and Schmidt-Rottluff. In the Netherlands we find Breitner, Verster, and Isaac Israëls working alongside the old Jozef Israëls, but likewise Toorop as representative of a new movement, while the first works of Sluyters and Mondriaan were soon to appear.
The beginning of the 20th century offers an attractive picture because of the great variety of movements and personalities producing their contributions to the development of modern art side by side. The great explosion which was to split painting into a number of movements had not yet taken place, but the old influence of tradition could, even at that time, scarcely keep back the flood of works and new ideas.

There were numerous attempts in those years to bring about a renewal of painting, and their starting points were often just as numerous. Seurat, who died in 1892 and whose work goes beyond impressionism, had already tried to base on the impressionist technique a firm, scientifically founded system and in this way to correct "arbitrariness" by the objectivity of science. A small *drawing* by him in our collection shows clearly how he succeeded in obtaining a great stability in the structure of the plane and thus

350

opened up a path which was to lead to a renewal of monumentality, to a new concept of the possibilities of wall painting. His striving for a new objectivity, for a structure of the painting which would be scientifically justified, represents one of the tendencies which, having begun before the turn of the century, was to determine art around 1900. The school of "divisionism" or "pointillism" has its origin in his work, and in the Netherlands and Belgium many artists, including Toorop, remained for a long period under the influence of this attempt at renewal.

Another school, which arose in France, also attempted to provide painting with a more objective basis, namely that of the Nabis. Our museum has one early work of this group namely *Vuillard's Interior*, but it is typical of the whole group. The painting is constructed on a triad of red, green, and white, and the painter has tried with these three colors to bind his subject in the plane of the painting and to derive a great decorative effect from it. The plane has regained its value and, with it, so has the decorative quality of the color and line which fills it. The result consequently resembles an arabesque.

358

There also took place in the Netherlands in these years a violent shift in social conditions which, in art, resulted in a reaction against impressionism and, in general, against a view of art based on a subjective attitude with regard to the material. The work of Jan Toorop took a decisive turn in these years. His portrait of Dr. Hendrik Muller, dating from 1901 (the first work purchased by the municipality of Amsterdam for the museum's collection), shows him to be still active in the style of impressionism. His Bluff-bowed Boat already shows how he had linked up with the striving for a more objective reproduction of nature as sought by pointillism. The same transition took place in *Verster's* work. After his "Peonies" he arrived in his *Three Pewter Mugs* at a consolidation of form. This more formal attitude can be clearly seen in the work of Thorn Prikker, the pioneer of monumental art which was then coming into being. The same tendency can also be felt in Belgium, where Rik Wouters—living in the Netherlands as a refugee since 1916—went through a similar development.

345

This striving for a consolidation of the plane and form—that is to say a reaction against impressionism—is seen most clearly in sculpture. The large, closed forms of Maillol's work, for example in the small *Bather*, which is cut in wood, and his bronze "The Night", are in clear contrast to the nervous, agitated play of forms in Rodin's plastic works. The revival of sculpture was taking place in the

352

SOIT
que

l'Abîme

blanchi
étale
furieux

sous une inclinaison
plane désespérément

d'aile

la sienne

par

338 stéphane mallarmé 1897

avance retombée d'un mal à dresser le vol
                    et couvrant les jaillissements
                            coupant au ras les bonds

        très à l'intérieur résume

l'ombre enfouie dans la profondeur par cette voile alternative

                    jusqu'adapter
                        à l'envergure

        sa béante profondeur en tant que la coque

                d'un bâtiment

        penché de l'un ou l'autre bord

painting and sculpture

339 g. h. breitner amsterdam 1893

340 **1887**

341 ± **1889**

342 **1901**

343 **1887**

g. h. breitner

344 tholen 1889

holland

345 verster 1904

poggenbeek ± 1895

348 thijs maris 1871

347 willem maris ± 1875

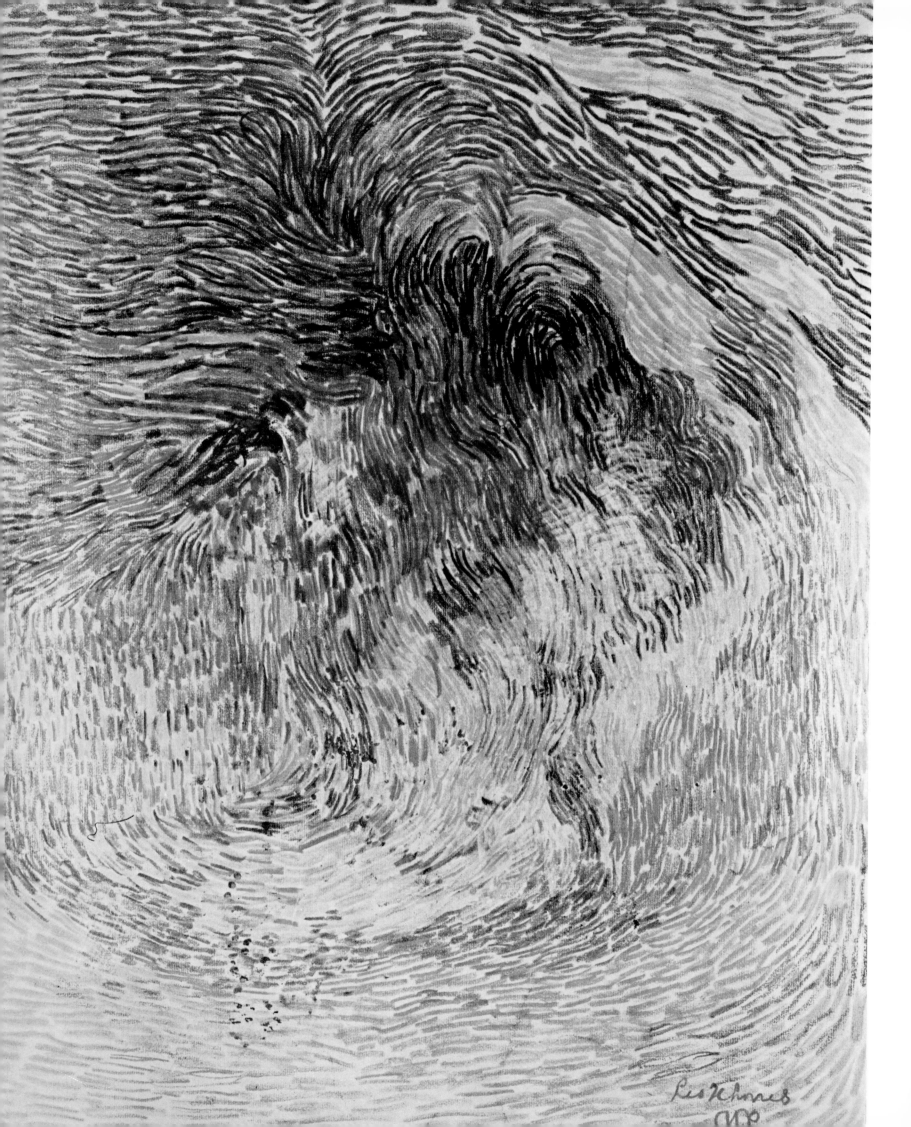

↑ 351 henri matisse 1900–1902   352 maillol ± 1900 ➡

353 auguste rodin 1898

↑ 354 maillol ± 1899   355 maillol 1896 ↑

← 356   odilon redon   ↓ 357   ± 1905

Netherlands during these years. Typical of it is the preference for a strict stylization in sculpture against a more flowing treatment of the forms in the plastic material. Mendes da Costa's "St. Anna" is a striking example of young Dutch sculpture, which arose in connection with *Berlage*'s revolutionary architectonic ideas.

It was in about 1890, when impressionism had just begun to find some recognition, that the first signs of a change in visual art became apparent. In a few works, human experience, rather than perceptible reality, began to inspire artists. "All that happened in the head and heart of man" became for the first time "more important than what man could perceive in his surroundings." This decisive step in the direction of another, of a new, art remains connected with the work of Cézanne, Gauguin, van Gogh, and Redon. These four painters are rightly considered the fathers and pioneers of a new art, although they had not yet taken the step which was later to separate art from perception. Their view of reality, their attitude with regard to perception, were nevertheless different from those which had existed, or, in fact, could have existed, before. The art of these "fathers of modern art" was scarcely appreciated while they were alive, and this fact too makes it clear that their works represented a new, revolutionary trend. Only later, after the turn of the century, was the time ripe, and the work of these painters was rediscovered by a young generation of artists. The passion of these younger artists, for whom the works of these pioneers became a source of inspiration, caused the movements in modern art to find their direction and new basis. It was precisely through the differences among these four great personalities at the end of the 19th century that modern art acquired its variety, its difference in direction and attitude with regard to reality.

Vincent van Gogh, whose work is, thanks to the kindness and devotion of his nephew V. W. van Gogh, represented very fully in our collection, is the first—although not the eldest—of the fathers of modern art. His work conferred direction and significance on expressionism. Vincent's work is, however, of primary importance because of his revolutionary strength, his deep humanity. The development of his work, from his beginning in the Netherlands up to the last canvases which were painted in France, can be seen in our collection, which shows the striving to give expression to the deep movings of human feeling, and finally the achievement, to an ever greater degree, of this aim. Vincent nevertheless begins from reality, and in this respect remains

faithful to the Dutch tradition. His early works prove how he followed the style of The Hague School. *The Potato Eaters* **382** his main work from this period, shows Vincent already on the path towards another, progressive art. In the heavy, somber color of his Brabant period he tried, by means of a piece of reality, to express those human feelings which form the basis of life. A sincere pity and a strong love for his fellow men incite him to do this, and although his painting was to change in the course of a few years, that need to give expression to his feelings of alliance to man and things always dominated his work. Vincent the man continues to show Vincent the painter the path, and that is perhaps the most revolutionary feature of his art—a feature which can be clearly discerned in his series of *Self-portraits*. **372** The path of van Gogh the painter is easy to follow in the museum from his paintings and drawings. He began in the footsteps of The Hague School, for, as a pupil in his uncle's art business, he had his own judgment about the art of his time and a preference for that school. Certain drawings already show that it was the need for expression and not skill which guided his hand. He then began to take lessons in painting in oils from his uncle Anton Mauve in The Hague. His paintings from this period are more influenced by his teacher and the work of The Hague School than are his earlier drawings. Soon there is, however, a break with Mauve, who disapproved of Vincent's feeling of independence and his general behavior. Vincent had in fact, from feelings of humanity and pity, taken a poor woman of the streets and her children into his house. After the break with Mauve, Vincent went to Drenthe, and there, in close contact with nature and the peasants, he began to find his own style, which he further developed and deepened after he had returned to his father's house at Nuenen. He wanted to become the painter of peasant life, and *The Potato Eaters* **382** clearly shows his striving and idea. He no longer tried, as did his predecessors of The Hague School, to provide a representation of a piece of reality in all its exactitude and with all the details, but he sought precisely those changes in reality which exclude what is fortuitous and consequently reveal so much better what is characteristic and typical. He sought an image of reality which—to use his own words—"is truer than the literal truth."

The Potato Eaters was preceded by studies and sketches. After completing this great work van Gogh strengthened his style, which had in its present form reached a climax. He went to Antwerp, and very soon after to Paris, where, under the influence of the impressionists, he was not long in finding another element of his art, that is, color. His palette became lighter, his touch livelier, more daring, and during his short stay of just two years in Paris he painted still lifes, landscapes, and the human figure which clearly show his increasing mastery of color. A painting such as the

379 Park at Asnières shows Vincent's Parisian style in its full maturity. His stay in that city and the impressionist technique were, however, for him but one school, one stage in his development. In 1888 he went to Arles in the south of France where he again discovered his own style. In the two and a half years which still remained to him, he continued to work uninterruptedly and in a feverish tempo,

373 producing such great works as The Sunflowers, the landscapes

376 around Arles, the portraits of friends, and later, in St. Rémy, the landscapes with the mountains in the background and the variations on paintings by Millet, Rembrandt, and Delacroix, and finally, in Auvers, the series

368 of landscapes in which he expressed the tragedy and loneliness which caused him to take his own life. All these works show the development of Vincent's own style and just as much also the growth of the artist as a man, since for him painting always remained a means for conveying a message to his fellow men, a testimony of the union between people, of being one with the objects in nature. Vincent therefore always began—as he wrote himself—by forming a careful and faithful idea of his subject, but this is by no means the end of his painting. In order to arrive at a high degree of expression he then exaggerated the colors and line, strengthening them, so that over and above the fortuitous element there arises a new, inner reality, a reality which is created by the feeling and mind of the artist. One of Vincent's great innovations was that he showed how animation and the inner union with man and the object were capable of renewing the view of reality and of reviving it. Vincent reintroduced human emotion, passion, and warmth into the painting of his time.

Alongside Vincent there stands as the other great innovator Cézanne, the man from the south of France, from the country which seemed to Vincent the promised land of painters. Cézanne in his innovations laid stress not on the emotional, subjective element, as the northerner van Gogh had done, but on the objective discipline of his mind. His art, which is never unduly intellectual, is unthinkable without the strict discipline and system which characterize the Latin mind. Cézanne was also set upon excluding fortuity from the design of a painting. Impressionism, from which he had proceeded, was to him too much an art for the eye which lacked any structure, any construction. He

tried to give back to painting its architectonic feeling and to find a firm construction for the new richness of color which impressionism had captured. Cézanne found this structure in the discoveries of the human mind, and particularly in geometry. It was he who said that every form in nature can be reduced to the cone, cylinder, and sphere. That strict construction, which he sought in each of his works, is also characteristic of the two paintings in our

395 collection, namely the landscape La Montagne Sainte Victoire, in which the mass of the mountain leads the painter to this geometrical arrangement, and the "Still Life", in which Cézanne arranges forms in order to create the geometrical theme for his painting by their contrast. It appears from both paintings that, however much Cézanne was attached to nature, it was not for him the theme itself which constituted the importance of the painting, but its "musical development" the way in which he succeeded with colors and forms in creating an entity with a new and personal richness. Cézanne freed painting of its dependence on the fortuities of nature by stressing the ordering procedure of the human mind.

His work links up with the great tradition of the Latin classical spirit, of which he is the modern master. Two other painters also belong to this group of "fathers of modern painting," namely Gauguin and Redon. Gauguin was the first to rediscover the world of the primitive races. In the seclusion of the Breton villages and on his voyages to the South Seas he found the simplicity of portrayal which still exists for the inhabitants of places which did not know 19th-century urban culture. Large, simple forms, wide planes of simple color lacking the refinements of scientific perspective placed in the plane, give his works the great, simple harmony which characterizes his paintings in our

364 collection, such as his Self-Portrait, and the portrait of his

363 friend Vincent while the latter was at work painting the Sunflowers. These canvases came from the collection of Vincent's brother Theo, the art dealer, and have been kindly made available by V. W. van Gogh, together with other documents relating to Vincent van Gogh's life, such as the

367 Self-Portrait by his friend Émile Bernard, which is dedicated to Vincent.

356 Finally we come to Redon, whose work is well represented in the Regnault collection. He was the discoverer of the world of dreams and the subconscious and consequently the father of surrealism. He discovered a reality which is not accessible to direct perception, namely the dream images of man, those strange agreements between color and

358   vuillard 1905

359   g. h. breitner ±1897

sound, form and perfume, which Baudelaire had first put into words as *correspondances*. A new world of forms becomes alive here—bizarre and sometimes capricious, not to be followed by alert reason, nevertheless compelling through the richness of associations and enchanting because of the radiant colors. Redon's pastels often seem as if they are illuminated from the inside, like church windows, by a mysterious brightness which has no visible source of light, a light such as sometimes shines in our dreams. Redon opened up for painting worlds which had not previously been discovered by the visual arts, and he pointed out new paths to his branch of art. During the same years *James Ensor* also penetrated the spectral nature of reality and—with an impressionist touch—created a sort of X-ray of reality. He is, with Redon, the master of the fantastic, having looked through the image of perception.

The four "fathers of modern painting" were scarcely recognized while they were alive and were certainly not adequately appreciated. This lack of appreciation is, however, perhaps a feature of modern art. These men saw further than their contemporaries and discovered a horizon for painting which was only later surveyed. These "fathers" were in their art still deeply rooted in reality, but they freed painting from a passive dependence on direct perception. They showed that man is not the slave of his eyes, but that it is the human mind in all its richness and variety which gives form to experience and which passes on this experience to fellow man. Each of the "fathers" opened up a different aspect of the human mind for painting, and only later generations have fathomed the importance of their discoveries.

The "fathers of modern art" are of such great importance to us because they broke through the dependence of art on perception and replaced it by another reality created by the human mind, that is, a truth which succeeds in giving form to human passion, the regulating mind, primitive simplicity, or the introverted dream.

The "fathers of modern art" all proceeded from the school of impressionism, but they quickly realized that certain features of impressionism represent for their view of painting just so many imperfections. They saw in impressionism the mastery, even the tyranny, of the eye in painting, and they tried to break this tyranny. Other painters who were their contemporaries nevertheless succumbed just as completely to this mastery of the eye, and they expressed in their works the attitude towards life

of their time. The impressionists in France and their followers in the Netherlands were just as much discoverers as the masters who, a little later, mastered the principles of impressionism.

In the Netherlands *Breitner* was working. Just a few years younger than Vincent van Gogh—the two were friends during the years that they lived in The Hague. It may well be said that Vincent van Gogh renewed European painting, but Breitner also made important discoveries for Dutch painting. The deep, universally human feelings which Vincent had contributed to the renewal of painting are scarcely expressed in Breitner's work (he is less revolutionary), but his eye, which was trained to an unprecedented degree of sharpness of perception, succeeded in discovering numerous features of everyday life, which typify its essence.

Breitner was the discoverer of Amsterdam, and that is one reason why his art is still dear to us today. He discovered the new, living Amsterdam and he expressed his vision of the city in a number of paintings in which the life of our city pulsates. Breitner's eye as a painter saw that the face of Amsterdam gets its character not only from the old façades, the gray, vaporous light and the heavy skies, but that the drays, the servant girls who hurry over the bridges, and the smoke from the barges along the quays are just as much part of the aspect of the city. To the features of the old city he added the characteristics of the living, working Amsterdam, and thus he was the first to discover its new face. Work and movement are always his preferred subjects, and he therefore felt attracted to streetscenes, to the work involved in opening up and building new districts. Amsterdam is for Breitner a pulsating, swarming mass of people, and he, the painter, stands in the midst of that mass. Breitner's view of Amsterdam is of such importance because he felt and expressed the revolution in the life of the city, a city which, in the second half of the 19th century, had awakened from a sleep, a city where also, for the first time in the Netherlands, the workers had become aware of their importance and their work, where the working class had begun to play a part in the life of the community and where incipient socialism had created an initial stronghold.

Breitner is represented—partly thanks to the gift by the "Society for the Promotion of the Maintenance and Spreading of a Public Collection of Contemporary Art in Amsterdam"—by an important series of works in our collection. Certain works create the impression of being exceptions in this general picture, for example, the quiet, pensive full-length "Self-Portrait", and the stately portrait 343 of *Mrs. Mann-Bouwmeester*, which creates an impression of inner suspense. The spirit and bustle of the 19th century nevertheless predominate in his other works. Breitner's sensitive eye succeeds in noting and recording every movement and every nuance of lighting. It was for him a question of continually expressing the movement, the 339 pulsating life of a large modern city. *The Dam in the Evening*, 359 the "View of the Dam", *Three Women on Board* and the 342 *View of the Lauriergracht* are examples of this effort, but his "piledriving work" is probably the masterpiece of the series. All the movement and bustle associated with a large building site and piledriving installations are expressed here within the range of a few colors, with a broad, lively touch, and the artist has succeeded in giving this harmony of gray, brown, and blue shades a further special touch by the vivid reddish-white of the surveyors' measuring sticks. All the details in this painting have been seen—and seen particularly sharply—but the painter has given his perception a separate significance, because these details were new and had not previously been seen. Breitner was consequently not only a painter with a sensitive eye and a lively touch— he was also a discoverer.

Certain other painters, mainly from Amsterdam, formed with Breitner the school which is sometimes called Dutch 346-344 impressionism. Isaac Israëls, *Poggenbeek* and *Tholen* are represented by characteristic works in our collection. Their work is impressionist in so far as their aim is to record and represent the fleeting impression, the moment- ary impression on the retina. They did not, however, master the technique and theory of impressionism. Vincent van Gogh is the only Dutch painter who worked strictly impressionistically during the years 1886 and 1887, because he was, through his brother Theo, in close contact with the masters of French impressionism.

These French masters did in fact raise the principle of the mastery of the eye in painting to its utmost height and they derived their theories and technique from this principle. On the basis of a new optical theory the impressionists no longer mixed their colors on the palette and then applied them mixed on the canvas, but they achieved the mixing of their colors in another way. They applied the unbroken colors unmixed and pure in small adjacent daubs on the canvas, so that the various neighboring colours mix in the observer's eye to give the desired effect. In this way the impressionists keep the purity and splendor of the unadulterated colors and still give each color its

desired nuance. They also achieve by this technique a sparkling of the color and a mobility of the surface which serve their purpose particularly well. They try to capture movement, the fleeting moment and even the most transitory element, such as the light, on their canvases. It is this effort to record the optical impression which gave this group of painters the name of "impressionists"—even if it was initially a nickname. The museum has only a few examples of really strict impressionism. There are two works by *Claude Monet*, who was also the leader of the 241 group—Claude Monet who was scarcely younger than Cézanne and several years older than van Gogh and Gauguin. His "Corniche de Monaco" is a typical example of impressionist technique, but also of the impressionist spirit, which liked to indulge in the fascination of color, line, and rhythm, without worrying much about what could be associated with this fascination. That fascination is in fact also passed on to the observer through the painting, which shows through the mobility of the touch even the vibration of the hot air on the colored rocks—the eye has reached here an extreme degree of sensitivity.

Apart from Monet's works, the museum also has a number of works which may certainly be classed with impressionism, even if the impressionist technique is not strictly applied in them. Both Degas and Toulouse-Lautrec tried to record the impression of the fleeting moment, even if both did it more through line than through the movement of color. In a number of drawings and studies, and even in small plastic works, *Degas* followed every movement of the female body, and this interest in movement caused him to choose subjects such as jockeys, dancers, and actresses. The few works in the museum's collection are striking examples of his power 362 of observation in which he tried to equal photography in exactness and detachment.

Toulouse-Lautrec's works in the collection show this artist's development from an impressionist technique— Woman at a Table and the absorbing *Portrait of van Gogh*—to his own 384 style, in which line and movement are the most important elements. His late works, of which the "Moulin de la Galette" and the *Violinist Dancla* are typical examples, 361 show the importance of this play of lines. Toulouse-Lautrec suggests the movement and instability of the moment, particularly through two elements in his work, namely the *mise en page*— that is, the strange, sometimes surprising, clipping from reality, in which bodies are cut by the frame of the painting and consequently appear to walk into and out of the painting—and the line, which has achieved the same mobility, the same sparkle and liveliness, as color

360   james ensor 1888

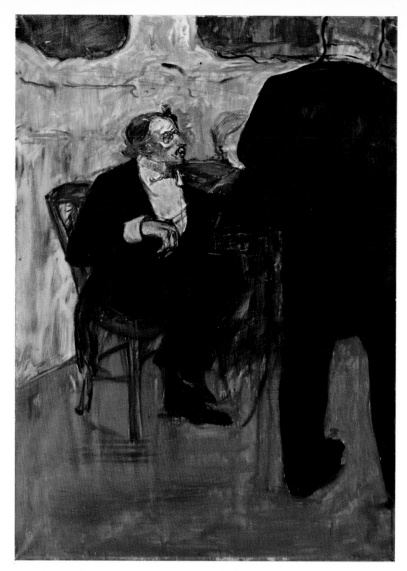

361 toulouse lautrec 1900

362 edgar degas 1890

364

365

366

367

3 hommages à van gogh:

364 'les misérables à l'ami vincent p. gauguin 8[8]

365 'à l'ami vincent c. laval 88'

367 'émile bernard 1888 à son copaing vincent'

366 vincent → theo 1888

vincent van gogh

368   auvers 1890

369   saint-rémy 1889

370   saint-rémy 1889

371   auvers 1890 ➡

375 vincent → theo 1888

374 arles 1888

376   arles 1888   377   paris 1888

378 paris 1887

379 paris 1887

380   paris 1887

381 nuenen 1885

382 nuenen 1885

drawings and pastels

: le blanc cru et dur d'un mur blanc
contre le ciel à la rigueur s'exprime
et d'une façon étrange par le blanc cru
et ce même blanc rabattu par un ton
neutre. Car le ciel même le colore
d'un ton lilas sur   blanchie entièrement
à la chaux (le local)

Encore dans ce   posée sur un terrain
paysage si naif   orangé certes car
lequel est sensé nous   le ciel du midi
représenter une cabane   et la méditerranée
bleu   provoquent un orangé d'autant plus intense
que la gamme des bleus est plus montée de ton

la note noire de la porte des vitres de la petite croix
sur la faite tout qu'il y a ait un contraste simultané
ressemble   bleu   une femme habillée
à l'oeil   d'une robe carrelée
tout   noir et blanc dans
autant que   le même paysage
celui du   orangé   primitif d'un ciel
bleu avec   bleu et d'une terre
l'orange   orangée. ce serait
Pour prendre   assez drôle à voir
un motif plus   je m'imagine
amusant   justement à Arles on
Supposons   porte souvent du carrelé
                           blanc et noir.

Suffit que le noir et le blanc sont des couleurs
aussi plutôt dans bien des cas peuvent
être considérées comme couleurs car leur contraste
simultané est aussi piquant que celui du
vert ou rouge par exemple.

385   vincent saint-rémy 1889–'90

386 saint-rémy 1889–'90

391   éduard manet ± 1880

392 toulouse lautrec ± 1890

393   edgar degas 1887

in Monet's work. Both try—one by color, the other through line—to record and suggest the transitoriness of the moment and the mobility of the optical impression. This art of the stirring, tense line found unprecedented possibilities in lithography and posters, two branches of the visual arts which Lautrec brought to rapid prosperity. The same striving for liveliness, for a suggestion of the moment, which inspired the impressionist painters also left its stamp on the sculpture of this period. It is striking and typical that *Rodin*—the great sculptor of that time—worked principally in clay and bronze (i.e., plastically), and not in stone, because he could in that way model the surface more vividly. Light and shade help to give his works, such as

318   *The Bearer of the Key*, the mobility he sought.

Side by side with the work of the recognized impressionist painters and sculptors, one finds in our museum works by a few artists who exerted a decisive influence on impressionism, for example *Édouard Manet* and *Johan Barthold Jongkind*. We have an extremely typical work by Manet, to wit the

394   sketch for the *Bar aux Folies Bergères*, a work in which we are struck by the liveliness and spontaneity of the touch and the rapid, telling manner of seeing, which at the same time show the importance of Manet as a forerunner of impressionism, of this art of the eye.

Jongkind, the Dutchman, was himself recognized by the impressionists as their forerunner, particularly because he introduced one of the most important innovations into France, such as the painting of landscapes in the open air.

396   His *Street in Névers* is an example of his impressionist style. Through his *pleinairisme* he contributed to that great refinement of the eye, that sensitivity to color and line, which must now be considered as the great acquisition of impressionism. Jongkind influenced French Impressionism, yet he came from a tradition which, at that time, certainly in France, already belonged to the past Romanticism. His early work shows his romantic sensitivity and at the same time the keenness of observation from which his later style evolved. Through his own observation Jongkind broke through the formula and scheme in which painting in his day threatened to suffocate.

The generation of "realists" also brought about a renewal in France. Courbet was their leader and the spirit of the 1848 revolution found expression in their work. Van Gogh speaks in his letters of how the humanity of the generation of 1848 and its honesty both inspired their art. Vincent felt attracted to this generation precisely because of its

humanity and simplicity. For it was the simplicity, the unaffectedness, which struck van Gogh in the Eighties and which strikes us now, and which was at the same time the new element and acquisition of that generation. This simplicity, obtained through a devoted observation of everyday objects, freed painting in those days of the danger of running aground in the representation of allegorical and historical scenes. It brought painters out of the world of stories and ideas back to the world around them, the world in which they themselves and their fellow men lived. Courbet, an artist who was aware of interpreting human values in an artistic language, created realism, or at least proclaimed it.

The depiction of contemporary reality was precisely the discovery of the realist school, and a series of works in our collection give a clear picture of its spirit. The simplicity and everyday nature of the object and of its portrayal are everywhere dominant, for a simplicity of objects goes with a clear aversion to the virtuosity of artistry.

The Dutch realist painters—the masters of The Hague School and their predecessors—were able to link up with the realist tradition of the 17th century. They were, however, inspired chiefly by their French contemporaries. The realism of the 17th century returned to the Netherlands indirectly via the Barbizon School. This Dutch realism of the second half of the 19th century is also principally landscape art—a rediscovery of the Dutch landscape with all its charm of cloudy skies and reflections. The masters of The Hague School did not, however, go as far in their observation as Jongkind had previously done. The atmosphere of the landscape was the foremost problem in their art. Only much later, towards the end of the century when impressionism had penetrated into the Netherlands, could Willem Maris say that he did not paint cows, but the light on their spotted coats.

The art of The Hague School was principally one of moods. It shows in this a greater relationship with the Barbizon School than with 17th-century Dutch realism. The three Maris brothers brought this 19th-century realism in painting to its greatest development. Their work is well represented in our collection. We have, thanks to the gift of the Society, an important series of works by Jacob Maris, the pioneer of the Hague School, which are outstanding because of the broad brush-stroke and his bold, energetic manner of painting.

By Matthijs Maris, the dreamy, poetic member of the
family, there is his masterpiece *Souvenir d'Amsterdam*, a
dreamy synthesis of all the typical Amsterdam corners
near the harbor, composed in a somber yellowish-gray to
form a vision, a remembrance, which tries to emerge
beyond reality.

Willem Maris, the youngest of the three, is represented
inter alia by his masterly *Winter Landscape*, which,
although an exceptional work, summarizes all the mastery
of the art of moods of The Hague School.

Besides these masters of the art of landscape, there were
two further important personalities in the Netherlands,
Jozef Israëls and August Allebé. Israëls originated
from romanticism, but in the Fifties his work was affected
by the spirit of 1848. Sympathy with the poor and the ideals
of humanity found a lively interpretation in his paintings.
His work is represented in our collection principally by the
late self-portrait of the patriarch of The Hague School,
dating from 1908. Finally we have Allebé's *Museum Visit*,
a vividly painted, slightly anecdotal work, which still
enthralls us today by its fine humorous observation, but
which stands out particularly through the difference in
atmosphere between a museum visit in 1870 and the present.
Not only the museum visit, but certainly the whole field
of visual art has changed completely in the ninety years
which separate the observer of today from the painter of
1870. Visual art has in this period of time turned more and
more clearly away from the sensory perception of reality
and has been directed towards the depiction of the essential
features and underlying structure, which are not directly
visible to the perceiving eye. This shift is based on the new
vision which the human mind has acquired in the last
century concerning the structure and laws of nature, and
also on new opinions about the processes of human thought
and feeling. All these discoveries and views have brought
with them a new notion of reality in visual art, a view
of the world around us and inside us, which no longer takes
any pleasure in the projecting of an existing, visible
reality, but which wishes, in addition, to make a communication about the importance to us of this reality. Visual art
in this century desires—to use a statement by Paul Klee—
not to reproduce the visible, but to make visible. It does
not desire to be a recognition, but a communication.
Visual art has, however, always been for man a path towards
a knowledge, a contemplation of himself and of the world
around him. That was the reason for a museum visit as
Allebé recorded it in 1870, and it is also the reason for it
today.   h. l. c. jaffé

394   éduard manet 1882

395   paul cézanne 1887

a museum in 1870

the museum as a tool

a large brick building (45,000 m³) which now can claim its pension (1895)

a new wing (6700 m³) in which much experience has been gained (1954)

two motion pictures a week, sunday afternoon-concerts, readings

40,000 children a year talking with 20 artists about art

radio-guided tours

may we now

present the museum   700 visitors a day

to you: 9000 subscribed groups

50 exhibitions a year   **architecture**   **motion picture**

in the building

50 outside of it   **photography**

20 catalogues a year

a museum monthly   **graphic arts**   **industrial design**

a study for graphic arts

a children's classroom   **painting**

a library

a reading room with 100 magazines   **sculpture**

a restaurant, a garden with works of sculpture

a reproduction shop   **typography**

with large reproductions, post cards, color slides

is it a beehive? a museum?

or very simply a meetingplace for the young and the old?

398   399   400   401   402

advertising

403

success

404

405

406 **sal meijer**

from 1945 to today

409 **1949**

410 **1950**

411 **195**

414 **terrace 1957**

from 1895–1940

407 **1938**

408

412 **1956**

413 **1960**

in the brick building of 1895

415 **restaurant 1957**

the blind

416

417

418

41

422 **expression**

420

exchanging impressions

421

423   424   425

new wing (1954)

426 **gonzales**   427   428

431   43

435   436   43

429

430 **new wing seen from the garden**

433

434 **picasso guernica**

438

439 **reading room**

442 **auditorium**

440 **reading room**

443 **auditorium**

441 **reproduction shop**

444 **auditorium**

some data

```
                                        s
                                       sss
        personnel 1960                sssss          staff
                                        s
                                        a
                                       aaa
                                      aaaaa          administration
                              aaaaa aaaaa aaaaa
                              PPPPP PPPPP PPPPP      technical personnel
                              PPPPP PPPPP PPPPP
                              PPPPP PPPPP PPPPP
                              PPPPP PPPPP PPPPP
                               PPP
                              wwwww                  cleaners
                              wwwww
                              vvvvv vvvvv vvvvv      inventory-taking
                               vvv
                                v
```

visits m = 10,000 visitors

```
1959  mmmmm mmmmm mmmmm mmmmm mmmmm
  58  mmmmm mmmmm mmmmm mmmmm mmmmm m
  57  mmmmm mmmmm mmmmm mmmmm m
  56  mmmmm mmmmm mmmmm mmmmm mmmmm mmmmm mmmmm mm
  55  mmmmm mmmmm mmmmm mmm
  54  mmmmm mmmmm mmmmm mm
  53  mmmmm mmmmm mmmmm mmmmm mm
  52  mmmmm mmmmm mmmmm m
  51  mmmmm mmmmm m
  50  mmmmm mmmmm
  49  mmmmm mmmmm
  48  mmmmm mmmmm m
  47  mmmmm mmmmm mmm
  46  mmmmm mmmmm
```

```
                          s      staff
                          ss
        personnel 1945    aaa    administration
                          PPPPP
                          PPPPP  technical personnel
                          PPPPP
                          PPPPP
                          w      workers/cleaners
                          www
                          w
```

between 1945 and 1960 the services of the municipal museums were enlarged with the following departments:
cabinet of prints
industrial design
modern photography
library
reading room
reproduction shop
bookkeeping
restoration studio
photo studio
inventory-taking
  department of all
  municipal possessions in the
  field of art